Foraging New England

Foraging New England

Finding, Identifying, and Preparing Edible Wild Foods and Medicinal Plants from Maine to Connecticut

Tom Seymour

Guilford, Connecticut
An imprint of The Globe Pequot Press

AFALCONGUIDE®

Copyright © 2002 by The Globe Pequot Press

All rights reserved. No part of this book may be reproduced or transmitted in any form by any means, electronic or mechanical, including photocopying and recording, or by any information storage and retrieval system, except as may be expressly permitted by the 1976 Copyright Act or by the publisher. Requests for permission should be made in writing to The Globe Pequot Press, P.O. Box 480, Guilford, Connecticut 06437.

Falcon and FalconGuide are registered trademarks of The Globe Pequot Press.

Text design: Lisa Reneson

Unless otherwise indicated, all photos are by the author.

Library of Congress Cataloging-in-Publication Data is available.

ISBN 0-7627-0954-5

Manufactured in the United States of America
First Edition/First Printing

The Globe Pequot Press assumes no liability for accidents happening to, or injuries sustained by, readers who engage in the activities described in this book

To my maternal grandmother,

Beatrice White

She had a love for nature and a sound knowledge of the healing powers of wild plants. Her memory is a constant inspiration for all who knew her.

Contents

Acknowledgments xi

Introduction xiii
> New England, the Forager's Paradise xiii
> Identifying Plants xiv
> The Forager's Tools xv
> Harvesting Techniques xv
> Toxic Plants xvi
> Poison Ivy, Biting Bugs, and Other Things to Watch For xvi
> Weather xviii
> Giardia xviii
> Medicinal Plants xviii
> Private Land xix
> Environmental Cautions xix
> Seasons xx

1 Plants of the Seashore 1
> Goose Tongue, *Plantago juncoides* 2
> Orache, *Atriplex patula* 5
> Sea Blite, *Suaeda maritima* 7
> Beach Peas, *Lathyrus japonicus* 9
> Sea-Rocket, *Cakile edentula* 11
> Glasswort, *Salicornia* spp. 13
> Silverweed, *Potentilla anserina* 15
> Northern Bay, *Myrica pensylvanica* 17
> Wrinkled Rose, *Rosa rugosa* 19

2 Plants of Fertile Streamsides   21

Ostrich Fern, *Pteretis pensylvanica*   22
Stinging Nettles, *Urtica dioica*   26
Curled Dock, *Rumex crispus* (also other *Rumex* species)   29
Wild Oats, *Uvularia sessilifolia*   31
Marsh Marigold, *Caltha palustris*   33

3 Plants of Disturbed and Cultivated Ground   35

Lamb's-Quarters, *Chenopodium album*   36
Quickweed, *Galinsoga ciliata* (also *G. parviflora* where available)   39
Field Peppergrass, *Lepidium campestre*   41
Green Amaranth, *Amaranthus retroflexus*   43
Purslane, *Portulaca oleracea*   45
Lady's Thumb, *Polygonum persicaria*   47

4 Woodland Plants of the Mottled Shade   49

Clintonia, *Clintonia borealis*   50
Indian Cucumber, *Medeola virginica*   52
Large-Leafed Aster, *Aster macrophyllus*   54
Bunchberry, *Cornus canadensis*   56
Wintergreen, *Gaultheria procumbens*   58
Purple Trillium, *Trillium undulatum*   60
Common Blue Violet, *Viola papilionacea*   62
Serviceberry, *Amelanchier* spp.   64

5 Mushrooms   67

Morel, *Morchella esculenta*   69
Chicken of the Woods, *Laetiporus sulphureus*   71

Hen of the Woods, *Grifolia frondosa*   73
Puffball, *Calvatia gigantea* (and other *Calvatia* species); Gem-Studded Puffball, *Lycoperdon perlatum*   75
Oyster Mushroom, *Pleurotus ostreatus*   78

6 Plants of Swamps, Bogs, and Slow-Moving Streams   81
Cattail, *Typha latifolia*   82
Pickerelweed, *Pontederia cordata*   85
Wild Cranberry, *Vaccinium macrocarpon*   87

7 Trees   91
White Pine, *Pinus strobus*   92
Eastern Hemlock, *Tsuga canadensis*   94
Red Spruce, *Picea rubens*   96
Willows (White Willow, *Salix alba;* Black Willow, *Salix nigra;* and other species of willow)   98

8 Medicinal Plants   101
Valerian, *Valeriana officinalis*   104
Sarsaparilla, *Aralia nudicaulis*   106
Yarrow, *Achillea millefolium*   108
Boneset, *Eupatorium perfoliatum*   110
Heal-All, *Prunella vulgaris*   112
Common Saint-John's-Wort, *Hypericum perforatum*   114
Canada Goldenrod, *Solidago canadensis*   117
Goldthread, *Coptis groenlandica*   119
Spotted Joe-Pye Weed, *Eupatorium maculatum*   121
Mugwort, *Artemisia vulgaris*   122

9 The Waste Places   125

Japanese Knotweed, *Polygonum cuspidatum*   126
Jewelweed, *Impatiens capensis*   129
Common Milkweed, *Asclepias syriaca*   132
Great Burdock, *Arctium lappa*   134
Orpine, *Sedum purpureum*   136
Evening Primrose, *Oenothera biennis*   138
Pineapple Weed, *Matricaria matricarioides*   140
Common Plantain, *Plantago major*   142
Wild Raspberries and Blackberries, *Rubus* spp.   144
Wild Strawberry, *Fragaria virginiana*   146
Highbush Cranberry, *Viburnum trilobum*   148
Sweetfern, *Comptonia peregrina*   150
Dandelion, *Taraxacum officinale*   152
Ground Ivy, *Glechoma hederacea*   155
New England Aster, *Aster novae-angliae*   157

10 Animals   159

Crayfish, *Decapoda astacus*   160
Bullfrog, *Rana catesbeiana*   163
Freshwater Mussels   166
Common Blue Mussel, *Mytilus edulis*   168
Periwinkle, *Littorina littorea*   171
Atlantic Razor Clam, *Ensis directus*   173
Surf Clam, *Spisula solidissima*   175

Glossary   179
Index   181
About the Author   186

Acknowledgments

Special thanks go to Jeff Serena, executive editor at Globe Pequot. It was he who saw the need for a regional, foraging series and it was he who asked me to pen this book. A host of other persons have supported and assisted me in my ongoing love for foraging. Among these are my friend Ken Allen, my grandpa, Tom White, and my friends John and Eleanor Avener.

Introduction

New England, the Forager's Paradise

Mountains, hills, rivers and streams, tidal rivers and seashores: New England's diverse geography is representative of what the rest of the country has to offer. Sandy plains, more typical of the West, are found here, too, as demonstrated in the vast "blueberry barrens" of Washington County, Maine. Deep swamps, as seemingly impenetrable as southern bayous, brim with fascinating plants and animals.

New England winters are noted for their severity, but the cold and snow of winter have benefits that, too often, people fail to appreciate. For instance, many beautiful and useful plants drop seeds that need stratification: that is, the seed must pass a season of below-freezing temperatures before it is ready to germinate when spring arrives. And even during the coldest, snowiest winters, the occasional balmy day lifts our spirits and calls us outside to check animal tracks in the snow, while enjoying a hot cup of pine-needle tea.

New England springs have about them an ephemeral quality. We try our best to capture the essence of spring—to sample all it has to offer—before it escapes. The first warm day in March releases earthy scents from recently thawed hillsides, scents that have not teased our senses since the previous fall. The urge to go out and search on the south-facing side of the house for the first spindly, fragile dandelions is too strong to resist. Maple sap drips from broken branches and insects, awakened from their long winter sleep, go about their business as if winter had never happened.

From spring through the first frosts of fall, New England offers a continually changing list of wild treasures. It is difficult for the forager to keep up with whatever is ready at the moment. Mostly we have our favorite species and take pains to be at the right place at the right time to harvest them; for the rest, it is catch-as-catch-can. New England literally has too much for the forager to sample in one lifetime.

Even those living in the northernmost section of New England are never much more than half a day's drive from the seashore. Here, on the sandbars, gravel, and rocks that make up the New England coast, are species that practically beg the forager to sample. The mountains, on the other hand, contain dozens of useful and interesting plant and animal species. Our rural New England roadsides have their own collection of edible and medicinal plants; even in the largest cities, vacant lots don't remain vacant for long, because plant invaders—usually desirable, edible species—quickly take up residence. Given all this, it is easy to see how New England and foraging go hand in hand. It really doesn't get any better than this!

Identifying Plants

While wild-plant harvesters need not be trained botanists, a basic knowledge of some of the more common terms used to describe plants is definitely in order. Plants do not retain the same physical features all season long. Some immature plants bear little resemblance to the adult or flowering plant. And yet certain traits are always present to set the plant apart from others and identify it. Shape of leaves and their arrangements, for instance, are important characteristics and must be considered in making a proper identification. Besides, wild plants have their dangers, and the only way to avoid using a toxic plant is to be absolutely assured of the plant's identification.

That aside, it's just plain fun to learn the basics of plant identification. To be unaware of the nature of the plants we see every day, to pass them by and not know their names, their uses, and their habits, is to live in a form of darkness. That darkness can easily be dispelled with a little study. The glossary in the back of this book will untangle the botanical terms necessary to identify wild plants.

Latin names are more specific and less ambiguous than common names, and very useful for identifying wild plants and animals. The system of Latin names we use today was developed centuries ago and still proves its worth. The Latin names of living things have two parts: genus and species. The first word in the name is the genus, and refers to the wider group to which the plant or animal belongs. Thus Evening Primrose, for example, belongs to the genus *Oenothera*. The second term in the Latin name is the species. It tells us something special about the plant to identify it exactly. Evening Primrose carries the species name *biennis,* which indicates that the plant is biennial, living for two years. The Latin name of Evening Primrose, then, is *Oenothera biennis,* sometimes abbreviated to *O. biennis.*

The Forager's Tools

Recreational foraging is almost virtuous in its simplicity. Specialized tools are definitely not needed, although a few basic hand tools, usually the common tools found in virtually every home workshop, barn, or garage, can make collecting easier. A typical recreational forager's arsenal of tools might include a hand trowel, jackknife, spade, and spading fork. Additionally, a pair of leather work gloves is always handy.

It is necessary to take something afield to hold the bounty. My favorite container is a handmade brown ash basket. Cloth bags are also good. Plastic bags tend to make plants go limp, and paper bags don't hold up well when it's wet outside.

And remember, if nature presents an impromptu bounty and no container is available, the mark of a true forager is an innate ability to improvise. Once, when I was pulling out of the parking lot in Bangor, Maine, my headlights illuminated a large patch of what appeared at first glance to be puffball mushrooms. A closer inspection proved that here, indeed, was a veritable bounty. But search as I might, no container could be found to hold the mushrooms.

Here was a difficult situation. This place was an hour's drive from my house, too far to make it worthwhile to drive home and return in the daylight, armed with bags and baskets. But this wasn't my first time around the track. I finally remembered that I did, indeed, have several suitable containers; I just hadn't realized it at first. Two spare jackets lay folded upon the backseat of my car. These could be spread out flat, the mushrooms piled on them and then wrapped up like a package for the trip home. Later, two bulging jackets held a year's supply of fresh, tender puffballs. A true forager is always prepared. And when we are not prepared, we can always improvise!

Harvesting Techniques

Picking plant matter need not harm the plant. Even plants that are relatively scarce (not threatened or endangered, but locally scarce) can be judiciously harvested without harm.

To harvest wild plants, always gather from a substantial group of plants, not from a small group of only a few individuals. Leaves, tender tips, and even stems can be snipped individually from one plant here, another plant there. This method actually encourages growth, just as pruning stimulates hearty growth on domestic plants.

Harvesting roots, tubers, or rhizomes is much the same. Concentrating only upon extensive plant colonies will, rather than harm the plants, stimulate lush growth.

Toxic Plants

Proper identification of all plants is critical. Did you know that some members of the parsley family are as lethal as the deadliest poison mushroom? It's true. Even a small nibble of Poison Hemlock *(Conium maculatum)* can kill. Other plants, such as White Baneberry *(Actaea pachypoda),* cause skin blistering, and when ingested, painful gastrointestinal difficulties. Still, other plants alter the heartbeat and blood pressure. And the list goes on. Should this cause the forager to refrain from dealing with plants? Absolutely not. It should, though, be ample cause to consult a field guide before as much as touching an unfamiliar plant. Better yet, take the field guide, or several field guides, out on foraging trips.

"Mushrooming," as some call it, is a popular, organized activity. Mushroom clubs abound in New England. After all, our area is prime mushroom habitat, thanks to our moderate, often moist climate. Nothing beats a field trip with a knowledgeable individual, and all it takes to find a group or club in the local area is to call the closest Extension service.

The best way for a beginner to proceed is to learn everything there is to know about one plant at a time. Learn it inside out, in all seasons. Then go to the next plant. Proceed with caution and a desire to learn. That's all it takes to become a safe, happy, and satisfied forager.

Poison Ivy, Biting Bugs, and Other Things to Watch For

"Leaves of three, let it be," run the words to a well-known verse. Poison Ivy and, to a lesser extent, Virgin's Bower or Wild Clematis have three divided leaflets, occur in New England, and are responsible for untold suffering, mostly in the form of severe skin irritations. Poison Ivy is sometimes difficult to recognize because its appearance varies. Virgin's Bower, while common and growing in dense colonies, is a climbing vine; oftentimes the unwary don't recognize it for what it is. Thus the value of the before-mentioned verse.

So how do casual visitors to the fields and woods manage to keep away from Poison Ivy and Virgin's Bower? The first and safest course is to stay on open paths and avoid coming into contact with any plants. But foraging requires some intimate contact with the green countryside, so the next best safeguard is to wear long-sleeved shirts and long pants and to bathe thoroughly upon returning home. Generally, this is enough to thwart any problems resulting from casual contact with poison plants. Jewelweed—which grows nearly everywhere and is described in this volume—not only is a good prophylactic, but also has properties that will soon dispel any rash that occurs, along with its accompanying discomfort.

Long pants and long-sleeved shirts are also good protection against biting insects, which, in New England, are legion. An insect repellent containing deet (diethyl toluamide) won't keep bugs from buzzing, but it will prevent insects from biting. In some instances repellents containing deet can cause allergic-type reactions. This is true in my own case, although coughing and sneezing, in my opinion, are less troubling than insect bites, which can become infected. Those who are sensitive to deet have little choice but to wear protective netting. The so-called green insect repellents containing citronella and pennyroyal, at least in my experience, do little to prevent insects from biting.

Deer ticks spread Lyme disease, a debilitating disease that is oftentimes difficult to diagnose. Again, try to stay on open trails as much as possible and wear long pants and long-sleeved shirts.

Bees can be a real problem. It is relatively easy to spot a paper wasp or hornet nest high in a tree. It is practically impossible to spot a yellow jacket nest, though. These mean critters have 1-inch-diameter escape and entrance holes in the ground, oftentimes at the base of a tree or shrub. Late summer and fall is the most dangerous time for these aggressive creatures. Not only are they more apt to swarm on a defenseless forager at that time, but my experience shows that they deliver a larger dose of venom, too. People who are allergic to bee stings must be vigilant. The only defense we have is to watch for yellow jackets entering and exiting, and to be sure we don't poke around the ground where any suspect hole exists.

Spiders are another story. These creatures lurk in dark places, crevices, corners, nooks, and crannies. Not much can be done to keep spiders from biting except to look first before inserting your hands or fingers in dark areas. Spiders are as much a threat in the home and garden as they are in the fields and forests. Even cold weather does not diminish the chance of an encounter. Once, while ice fishing on a particularly cold and windy day, the wind swept a large, and very much alive, spider across the ice in front of me.

Poisonous snakes are present in New England, except for Maine. However, these are pit vipers (copperheads and rattlesnakes) and hunt mostly at night. In states other than Maine, it is good policy to watch where you put your hands when climbing in ledgy areas and to scan the trail ahead of you for snakes. Generally, snakes are not a threat to foragers who exercise normal caution. In fact, pit vipers are scarce and in need of protection, so if you sight one, please leave it be.

Weather

Thunder and lightning signal danger. As soon as distant thunder is heard, it is time to quit foraging and head for safety. Do not stand near any large tree. And do not stand in the open. A motor vehicle is relatively safe because the rubber tires act as a ground; just don't touch any metal parts. Lightning is a very real threat not just in New England, but everywhere.

Giardia

In addition to the safety issues surrounding the eating of wild plants because of possible toxic side effects, a word about giardiasis, commonly called giardia, is in order. Giardia is an infection of the small intestine caused by the *Giardia lamblia* protozoan. Contaminated water is the culprit; beavers (giardia is also known as "beaver fever") and muskrats are carriers, and raw sewage leaching into waterways also tends to spread the protozoan. Drinking suspect water is always dangerous, but giardia can also be spread by other means. It is my contention that a certain danger is present when consuming aquatic plant matter from suspect water. Because of this threat, rinse plants thoroughly in clean water before eating them.

Medicinal Plants

It is greatly rewarding to go outside and pluck a plant, take it inside, steep it in water, drink the resulting tea, and gain relief from minor discomforts. It is dangerous, however, to consider plant medicines as anything but gentle helpers for minor complaints. Failure to consult qualified medicinal practitioners can lead to more severe illness or even death.

Private Land

Although the world is, proverbially speaking, "our blueberry," we foragers must operate within certain bounds. It is unlawful to forage upon land owned by another, without permission. Additionally, some public lands prohibit picking any plant matter. It is therefore imperative that you consult local regulations before picking any plant or capturing any animal. You must always secure permission when venturing upon private lands. And to those who would say, "But I know that the landowner isn't going to pick this stuff, so I might as well," I can only reply: "I understand. Nonetheless, we must still secure permission beforehand. Not only does common courtesy demand it, but it is also the law."

Environmental Cautions

Freshwater mussels, amphibians, plants, reptiles, and insects all share a common thread: Many of them are endangered, threatened, or of special concern. Fortunately, the current trend toward appreciation of nature and the desire to learn more about the natural world around us has illuminated the plight of these living creatures.

Foragers are in an enviable position: They are outdoors throughout the different seasons and so can observe the status of the creatures and plants in their own circle of travel. Such observations contribute to the bulk of knowledge about formerly little-known creatures and plants. Organizations such as Frogwatch USA (details are given in the chapter on bullfrogs: see page 163) gather data on amphibians from amateur naturalists. The Maine Department of Inland Fisheries and Wildlife recently conducted an extensive study of freshwater mussels and has published a book (noted in the chapter on mussels; see page 166) that gives lots of information on the status of mussels not only in Maine, but throughout New England as well. And hometown newspapers throughout New England now run nature columns, written by professional and amateur naturalists who outline important environmental issues.

As we become involved in nature, we become more a part of it. And as such, we will begin to work with, not against it. Being environmentally responsible requires commitment. Foragers are, and should be, at the forefront of the national awakening to the importance of our natural world and all the creatures that swim, fly, walk, creep, and crawl in and on it.

Seasons

Spring, summer, and fall are times of great activity for the forager. From the day in March when the first tender, green shoot pokes out from the forest litter, to fall when the last killing frost draws a distinct and final close to the growing season, foragers have more to do, learn, and observe than they have time for. Each season brings with it its delights, joys, and bounty.

It is important for foragers to understand the concept of what I call "mini seasons." Nothing remains the same in nature for more than a brief, fleeting instant. Plants do not appear the same from one month to the next. And each plant has its prime time for harvest or appreciation. The four seasons can, therefore, be divided up into lots of brief segments, or mini seasons.

For example, even before the ground is fully thawed in spring, the Evening Primrose is present along dirt roads and gravel lanes, ready for harvest. The flat, basal rosettes of the plant are—at that time and for that short time only—good for use in salads or as cooked vegetables. The roots, too, are edible, but again only for a short period. When the warm rays of the spring sun cause the outspread leaves to pick up and reach for the sky, the root becomes pithy and inedible and the leaves become tough. Later in late summer and early fall, the blooming plant bears little resemblance to the small, green- and red-tinted bunch of tender leaves seen along the roadside in early spring.

The Evening Primrose points out the value of recognizing the mini seasons. Each of these tiny slices of time can be recognized by the state of the various wild plants. Other factors contribute to the mini seasons. Spring peepers, wood frogs, and common toads can be heard at night, calling in the swamps and wetlands. This, too, lasts for only a brief interval. Bird arrivals—the warbler migration in particular—come on fast and are soon over, many of the birds having only stopped for a few days on their way north. Knowing the signs of the seasons contributes greatly to the forager's enjoyment and appreciation of nature.

Finally, winter is the time to relax, study, read books, and enjoy the wild harvest. Never do common dandelions taste better than when nor'easters howl and roads are plugged with snow. A cup of herbal tea made with foraged plant leaves or flowers imparts a warm glow to the spirit. The medicinal plants, dried and safely stored, are ready to combat the simple cold. By these means, the forager has managed to save a bit of the previous season. This is what helps us bear up until the following spring, when that first wood frog heralds the new season and a renewal of life.

～1～

Plants of the Seashore

The New England shore is home to a wide variety of edible plants and animals. And strange as it may seem, edible seaweeds cannot be listed among the numbers of easily gathered foodstuffs; most of these are available only along the bold coast, where depths plunge precipitously. A boat is usually necessary to gather edible seaweed, and even then it's not convenient except during extreme low tides. But a host of other ready-at-hand foods exist to delight and tantalize any forager willing to learn the ways of the seashore. What's even better, the seaside plants grow not only on the actual coast, but along tidal rivers and streams as well. A forager can find good pickings almost anyplace where the tide rises and falls.

The well-defined line of demarcation between the shore and the inland zones is of great interest to the forager. Plants that only grow inland are found scant inches from the extreme high-tide zone, and plants that only grow where they can be touched by sea spray grow tantalizingly close to the upper extremes of the beach. In New England our planting zones, as illustrated in the seed catalogs, are often vague and nondescript, but the seashore and the inland zones are practically carved in stone. The best of both worlds can be found here side by side.

Seaside foragers need to be aware of one caveat: Many of our more popular beaches have become favorite spots for people to walk their dogs. Given what dogs are fond of doing on plants, it may be advisable to limit wild-food gathering to the more secluded and out-of-the-way stretches of seashore.

Goose Tongue
Plantago juncoides

Color plate: Figure 1

Synonyms: Seaside Plantain, shore greens

Use: Cooked vegetable, salad ingredient

Range: Seashores throughout New England

Similarity to toxic species: Goose Tongue has a vague similarity to Arrowgrass *(Triglochin maritima)*. Differences are considerable, however. The leaves of Arrowgrass are fairly thin, whereas those of Goose Tongue are much wider and softer. And the succulentlike Goose Tongue leaves have an obvious groove. The straight leaves of Arrowgrass are primarily upright, while those of Goose Tongue are sometimes twisted at crazy angles and tend to droop; often a few leaves are prostrate. Arrowgrass is primarily a threat to cud-chewing animals.

Best time: Late May through August

Status: Common

Tools needed: None

Goose Tongue is related to the Common Plantain (see page 142). The difference between the two is in the leaves; common plantain has wide leaves with prominent veins, while Goose Tongue has slender, fleshy leaves. Also, Goose Tongue leaves have a deep indentation their entire length. A cross section of one of the 4- to 8-inch leaves would look like the cross section of a common house gutter. The seed stalk is shorter than that of the Common Plantain, rarely exceeding 10 inches. Goose Tongue usually grows in dense colonies, ranging from slightly below to slightly above the high-tide line. Sometimes, though, especially on rocky, inhospitable shores, resident Goose Tongue plants grow singly.

    Goose Tongue gets its name, naturally enough, from its similarity to a goose's tongue. Anyone who has ever been chased by an angry goose (don't laugh; once a family in Maine had such a mean goose that they had to erect a sign reading: DANGER, ATTACK GOOSE.) will note the likeness to a slender, pointed Goose Tongue.

Goose Tongue is one of those plants that are common, widespread, and yet go unnoticed by the vast majority of visitors to the seashore. Once, Goose Tongue was a New England favorite, ranking in popularity with dandelions and fiddleheads. But over the last fifty years or so, the folks who so favored this ubiquitous vegetable have passed on and few, if any, have stepped in to perpetuate the tradition of walking to the shore to pick a "mess of shore greens." The paucity of adherents, however, has no bearing on the goodness or worth of this flavorful plant. Indeed, Goose Tongue is sweet and mild, with just trace of saltiness.

Although Goose Tongue is common and abundant, it won't remain so if we harvest it indiscriminately. The trick is not to pull the plant up by its roots. Rather, the individual leaves should be trimmed. This is easily accomplished by snapping them with thumb and forefinger, like a fresh, crisp green bean. And it's good policy to take only the largest leaves from a plant, leaving the smaller leaves to grow and sustain the plant.

Not everyone has my good fortune to live so near the seashore. My grocery shopping sometimes consists of a visit to the store for bread and staples and a stop at the local Goose Tongue bed on the way home. Steamed Goose Tongue, along with whatever is in season in my vegetable garden, is a common summertime meal at my place.

Goose Tongue cooks quickly. It can be steamed or boiled. If boiled, use a scant amount of water; the leaves need not be covered. Boiling any green this way is similar to steaming in a commercially made food steamer. Once the leaves darken (the same way some green beans darken when cooked) and become limp, drain the greens and serve. A bit of butter and a lick of ground pepper go well with Goose Tongue. Some enjoy a dash of cider vinegar. My suggestion is to sample the greens first, sans vinegar, and then, if desired, try a splash of vinegar. Watch the salt, though. Even after thorough rinsing in fresh water (a must for all greens, especially those from the seashore), Goose Tongue retains a slight salt taste.

Some people like their shore greens in a salad, either in addition to other ingredients or as the main ingredient. Either way, the leaves should be chopped first. The easiest way to accomplish this is to use scissors, as when cutting chives.

Finally, Goose Tongue makes a superior frozen vegetable. Blanch the greens in boiling water, drain, and immediately drop them in ice-cold water to cool. When thoroughly cooled, drain the greens again, put them in freezer bags, and the job is completed. Frozen Goose Tongue easily lasts a full year in the freezer. It pleases me no end to sit in my tiny kitchen and watch the nor'easters howl outside while dining on steamed Goose Tongue. I can think of no finer way to re-create the essence of summer!

Orache
Atriplex patula

Color plate: Figure 2

Use: Cooked vegetable, salad ingredient

Range: Widespread above the high-tide line along the entire New England seacoast

Similarity to toxic species: None

Best time: June through September

Status: Common and plentiful

Tools needed: None. Orache is easily picked by hand.

Another member of the goosefoot family, Orache is a generally symmetrical, bushy plant—although sometimes plants growing in shade, or windswept, bare spots, are scrawny and prostrate. It can grow to 2 feet in height. The leaves are the key to identification. Roughly similar to leaves of Lamb's-Quarters (see page 36), Orache leaves have fewer teeth. In essence, the leaf is shaped like an arrowhead, with the "barbs" pointing out to the side. The leaf, especially the bottom, is coated with a grainy-feeling powder that can be wiped off with the fingers. The insignificant flowers grow in the leaf axils.

Orache leaves are easily stirred into motion by the slightest sea breeze when, like quaking aspens, they expose their light-colored undersides. This habit makes them easy to identify, even from a great distance. Of all the wild seaside vegetables, Orache is the most dependable; it is literally everywhere, no matter if the beach is rocky or muddy, gravelly or smooth.

Orache prefers the immediate high-tide line, often growing among, around, and through the various clumps of driftwood, dried seaweed, and other types of flotsam found there. No seaborne material, no matter how dense, seems able to smother the hardy and determined Orache.

A handmade brown ash basket is my favorite container when picking Orache. Placing the leaves and tender tips (the stems are edible, too, as long as they are tender and thin) in a bag seems to compact them, making them more difficult to separate for rinsing later. If the weather is hot and humid, my Orache leaves go into an ice-filled cooler upon returning to the car. Wild vegetables should be well cared for, just like fresh fish, from the time they are gathered until they reach the table.

Orache has a sweetness akin to the most tender young spinach, but none of the strong aftertaste associated with spinach. Orache does, however, have a distinctly ethereal dimension to its flavor, something best appreciated in the manner of a wine taster sipping, then breathing through the nose. Take one forkful of Orache, slowly chew and swallow, and, before taking another bite, examine the flavor sensed on the back of the tongue.

Orache is a big hit with participants in my seaside wild-plant walks. We usually try to pick and identify enough plants to provide a wild-food meal upon returning to my place. Orache, being the most abundant, yields an immediate reward for the first-time forager. It is easy to pick a basket- or bagful in short order. And though everything is new and different to most of these folks, it is the Orache that elicits the most comments at the end of the meal.

Here's something interesting. Some years ago a local plant company offered Orache seeds in its annual cataloge. Although this wasn't exactly the same Orache as grows by the sea, the company included a glowing description of the sweet flavor. It seemed to me a good idea to try and grow this cultivated Orache at home, in order to circumvent the short drive to the seashore. But the stuff didn't grow well, was highly prone to insect infestation, and, most important, didn't taste nearly as good as the "real thing." Sometimes we really can't improve on nature.

Pick the leaves and tender stem tips, rinse, and drop in a little boiling water. Cook until the Orache becomes dark, like spinach. Use plenty of fresh Orache to begin with, because it loses its bulk in cooking. Drain well and serve with butter, salt, and ground black pepper. Some may want to try cider vinegar on steamed or boiled Orache, but I don't care for that variation—it tends to cover up the fine flavor of the plant.

Orache freezes well. Blanch, cool, drain, and place in plastic bags for freezing. No store-bought frozen vegetable can compare.

Sea Blite
Suaeda maritima

Color plate: Figure 3

Use: Trail nibble, cooked vegetable, salad ingredient

Range: All of the New England seashore, near the high-tide line

Similarity to toxic species: None

Best time: June through August

Status: Common and abundant

Tools needed: None

Drifts of bluish green Sea Blite dot the upper reaches of most beaches. A member of the goosefoot family, Sea Blite can live in gravel, in sand, and even among rocks and boulders. A spreading plant, soft and vinelike, Sea Blite rarely stands more than a foot tall. More often the individual branches hug the ground. The tiny, alternate leaves are round and pointed, reminding the landlubber of any of the various species of spruce. But unlike spruce, Sea Blite is not prickly. Instead, it is soft and tender, succulentlike. Sea Blite has tiny yellowish green flowers tucked in the leaf axils.

Most foragers like their Sea Blite boiled or steamed. While it is indeed a fine potherb, it has several other uses that should not be overlooked. First—and this is an unorthodox use—Sea Blite is a superior trail nibble. The tender tips, stems, and leaves are great to chew on while walking the beach, searching for other seaside edibles. Sea Blite is quite salty, especially raw. But it isn't as salty as, for instance, salted peanuts, potato chips, or any of the popular jerky products. Why the slight taste of salt in raw Sea Blite is offensive to the same people who pay good money for highly salted junk foods is a mystery to me. And salt in Sea Blite, being sea salt, is full of necessary trace elements, as opposed to common table salt, which may contain only added iodine—or may not.

Sea Blite is easily picked by snapping the vinelike branches with the fingers. By picking only a few sprigs from each plant, it is possible to impart a manicured look to the plants without doing any harm whatever. Again, be sure not to pull Sea Blite up by its roots.

Rinsed, chopped Sea Blite makes a perfectly good boiled vegetable. It cooks fully in about ten minutes. Some authorities recommend cooking in two waters to remove the salty taste. That salty taste, though, is what makes Sea Blite stand out among the seaside vegetables. To attempt to circumvent entirely the salt taste is kind of like cooking rhubarb stalks in so much sugar that none of the tart, mouth-puckering flavor remains. It is the tartness, after all, that makes rhubarb so unique. And so it is with Sea Blite—salt fanciers take note.

A bit of chopped Sea Blite adds an interesting, pleasant dimension to any salad. Rinse, cut in small bits with kitchen shears, and sprinkle over the salad.

Perhaps the most oddball (and incidentally my favorite) use of Sea Blite is in a seaside stir-fry. Used alone or with any of the seaside edible plants mentioned here, Sea Blite comes alive in a hot wok. The ratio of one plant to another is entirely a matter of personal choice and, of course, availability. But no matter. Some things are best when not reduced to ounces, cups, and teaspoons. The pure off-the-cuff seaside stir-fry is a thing of beauty, a one-of-a-kind work of art.

My idea of heaven on earth goes something like this: Drive to the shore and pick a good assortment of whatever seaside veggies are in season. With the vegetable portion of the meal safely stowed, the next step is to gather about three pounds of blue mussels. The briny harvest is taken home, the mussels steamed, the vegetables stir-fried, and all is enjoyed outside, under the shade of the huge, whispering white pines behind my little cottage. Kings, princes, and potentates may have the money to buy better fare, but truth to tell, where could they find better than the homey, free seaside meal just described? The forager's life is sprinkled with earthly pleasures.

Beach Peas
Lathyrus japonicus

Color plate: Figure 4

Use: Cooked vegetable, trail nibble

Range: Widespread along the entire New England coast, slightly above the high-tide line

Similarity to toxic species: Beach Pea bears a slight resemblance to Vetchling, *L. palustris.* Vetchling generally, but not always, has a winged stem, as does its relative, that favorite shrub of landscapers, Euonymus. The Beach Pea is easy to differentiate from other members of the *Lathyrus* genus, however, because it produces peas in pods that are identical in every way to cultivated peas, except that they are tiny.

Best time: June through July

Status: Common and widespread

Tools needed: None

The Beach Peas is a vining plant, with leaves that can be either opposite or alternate. In my part of Maine, most Beach Peas have opposite leaves and are easily identified because the leaves, rather than splaying out, are held up, nearly touching each other. The showy, pealike flowers range in color from purple to pink and violet. The fruits are borne in seedpods that look like miniature garden pea pods.

    Beach Peas have a definite mystique. They are not pushovers, in that they are at their peak of ripeness for only a short time. Sometimes it takes many trips to the Beach Pea bed to determine when the peas will be ripe. And as often as not, something comes up, our nonforaging lives interfere, and by the time we return to pick the Beach Peas they are gone by, tough and insipid. But that is what makes them so hauntingly desirable.

    Barring the luxury of being able to visit the Beach Pea stand periodically, it helps to keep records, much the same way canny gardeners keep track of the first and last frosts, when the first tomato comes off ripe, and when the first mess of peas is ready. But the seasons in New England are notorious for being unpredictable. And *unpredictable* is a fit term to describe Beach Peas.

For all that, Beach Peas have another trait that makes them less than popular among visitors to the seashore: The individual peas are so tiny it takes an unduly long time to shell enough for a good meal. That said, it is important to remember that the more effort a project requires, the more the finished product is appreciated.

Beach Peas impress me with their tenacity. One of my old favorite Beach Pea stands is on a rocky, windswept slope. Here the pea vines twine around huge boulders and among giant timbers from long-forgotten piers that succumbed to some ancient hurricane. How anything can thrive in this repressive environment is beyond me. But the Beach Peas do. What's more, they seem to like it!

Once, the youngsters in our foraging group became enthralled with Beach Peas. The peas, happily, were at the peak of perfection, and the kids picked a colossal bunch. We adults made it clear that it would be their job to shell the peas upon returning home. Surprisingly, the children tackled the job and stuck to it like troopers, without complaining once. When the full wild meal was served, the kids got first crack at the boiled Beach Peas. I'm sure they were no better than any other peas these youngsters had tasted, but their hands-on experience made all the difference in the world. What a great lesson in cause and effect and the value of diligence.

Because Beach Peas lose some of their sweetness when cool, it is best to serve them hot. When preparing a complex meal, save the Beach Peas for last. When everything is nearly done, pour the shelled peas into boiling water and cook for about ten minutes. Serve immediately.

Fresh Beach Peas, at the height of ripeness, are pretty good raw, as trail nibbles. When the peas go past their prime, however, and the pods turn yellow and become tinted with red streaks, the peas become tough and insipid, better suited as ammo for pea shooters than as table fare.

Beach Peas can certainly be frozen, but who would want to bother? Take my advice and eat Beach Peas fresh, on the day they are picked. Then they can become part of an annual ritual, the Beach Pea feast. Little things like this are all-important pieces in the great puzzle that is the forager's year.

Sea-Rocket
Cakile edentula

Color plate: Figure 5

Use: Trail nibble, cooked vegetable, salad ingredient

Range: Widespread at or above the high-tide line along most of the Atlantic coast, including all of New England

Similarity to toxic species: None

Best time: June through August

Status: Common and plentiful

Tools needed: None. Sea-Rocket is easily picked by hand.

Sea-Rocket, a member of the mustard family, is found just above the high-tide line. Its sprawling habit, as well as its dark green, fleshy leaves and succulent stems, make identification easy.

The shiny, smooth, leathery-looking leaves have irregular, coarse teeth with few, if any, sharp edges. The tiny purple or blue flowers have four petals, each one cleft at the end. They appear in summer, followed by the distinct, two-parted seedpods that mark the beginning of the end of the season for this estimable seaside plant.

That Sea-Rocket is one of the mustards is made convincingly evident by its piquant taste. This sharp flavor is not at all unlike the hot mustard paste served in Oriental restaurants. Which is why those who enjoy hot mustard should make every effort to become acquainted with Sea-Rocket and those who dislike the mustard flavor are advised to give it a wide berth.

As a trail nibble (for mustard lovers, that is), Sea-Rocket excels. It ranks high among my favorites. My fondness for fresh Sea-Rocket is such that my passing along the beach can be marked by the great destruction wreaked on the youngest and most tender Sea-Rocket plants. Too much Sea-Rocket can trigger mild indigestion, I have found. That's a small price, though, for such a heady indulgence.

Besides nibbling the tender stems, terminal ends, buds, flowers, and seedpods straight from the plant, Sea-Rocket can be finely cut and added to salads. Using only a small amount will impart a flavor that is well defined, yet not overpowering. And uninitiated guests may wonder, but they will never guess the source of this clean, interesting flavor.

Sea-Rocket can be boiled for ten minutes for a fine vegetable. The cooking process dissipates some of the pungency. Serve drained Sea-Rocket with salt, pepper, and perhaps butter.

A better use for Sea-Rocket is as an addition to a stir-fry. In midsummer, when Purslane is altogether too abundant in my vegetable garden, I like to combine a small handful of chopped Sea-Rocket with a cup or more of chopped Purslane and quickly stir-fry the two over high heat. Sweet and sour sauce and soy sauce are optional; Oriental mustard is definitely not needed.

Glasswort
Salicornia spp.

Color plate: Figure 6

Use: Trail nibble, salad ingredient

Range: Widespread along the New England seacoast, tidal rivers, and streams

Similarity to toxic species: None

Best time: June through September

Status: Common

Tools needed: None. Glasswort is easily picked by hand.

Glasswort grows in dense colonies, always where it can be touched by extreme high tide and sometimes where it is regularly immersed. A member of the goosefoot family, glasswort is interesting to observe throughout the growing season because the change in appearance, as the plant matures, is so dramatic. As opposed to, say, a tomato—which even as a seedling has all the characteristics of an adult—immature glasswort plants resemble single, naked nubs. As the season progresses, glasswort (remember that since glasswort grows in massive colonies, the change is not so much a singular event as it is a mass occurrence) gains height as it sprouts branches. The overall effect is like a bed of moss slowly transforming into a forest of fir trees. And while, in the early season glasswort sports shades of brilliant lime green, toward the end of summer the shading turns to olive drab and, finally, to orange.

Look for glasswort beginning in July, when the plants are 4 or 5 inches tall (glasswort can reach a height of 12 inches, but that is toward the end of the season). Earlier, they are not worth picking. The two glassworts of most value to New England foragers are Dwarf Glasswort, *S. bigelovii*, and Slender Glasswort, *S. europaea*. The differences between the two are that Dwarf Glasswort branches are relatively short and stubby, while Slender Glasswort has longer, more slender branches. Note that some plants may never develop branches, remaining as solitary, slender spikes the entire season. Glasswort flowers grow in the joints of the plant; they are tiny and hardly noticeable.

A third variety, Woody Glasswort, *S. virginica,* exists in southern New England but the dwarf and slender types are better suited to the forager's needs. In northern New England the forager is more likely to encounter the dwarf variety.

Glasswort is, to my mind, a dinosaur, primitive and ancient. But my fascination with this admittedly weird-looking plant doesn't end with its physical characteristics. Its salty-sweet flavor beckons me to stop, find a comfortable place to sit or recline, and graze for a while.

The serious nibbler should select the most tender tips and branches. These are quite brittle and snap easily between thumb and forefinger. Foragers wishing to indoctrinate others into the myriad pleasures of foraging should select glasswort as the initial wild plant. No one, in my experience, has ever responded in other than a positive manner when first sampling glasswort.

For home use, glasswort can be cooked for ten minutes and served as a hot vegetable. But why cook a plant that is so utterly delicious raw? Far better to nibble the fresh plant at the seashore and pick some more to take home to use as a salad. Such a salad may be wholly composed of glasswort, or the glasswort may be mixed with other seaside goodies. Imagine a combination of Sea Blite, glasswort, Sea-Rocket, Orache, and Goose Tongue. Sprinkled with some balsamic vinegar and topped with freshly ground black pepper, this seaside potpourri could make you a legendary forager in your own time!

Silverweed
Potentilla anserina

Color plate: Figure 7

Use: Cooked vegetable, trail nibble

Range: Common locally throughout New England, Silverweed prefers rocky, gravelly shores, at or somewhat below the high-tide line.

Similarity to toxic species: Silverweed leaves bear a slight resemblance to tansy, which contains a toxic oil. The forager should encounter no difficulties, though, because tansy is an upright plant, while Silverweed bears prostrate stems.

Best time: July through September

Status: Common

Tools needed: While the edible roots can be harvested by digging with the fingers, a garden trowel or three-pronged, handheld weeder is recommended.

Silverweed, a member of the rose family, sports leaves that are silvery underneath. They are divided, with coarse, sharp-toothed leaflets that grow opposite each other, with the larger leaflets on top and the smaller near the base. The yellow flowers have five petals. The white roots are shiny and fleshy.

The Silverweed on my local seashore grows in the most difficult areas to harvest: the sharp gravel between rocks and boulders. This is not so everywhere, thankfully. Still, given my situation, a handful of Silverweed roots, harvested with the hands, represents lots of hard work. It seems I never remember to carry a digging tool.

Because of the difficulty (for me) involved in harvesting a good supply of Silverweed root, I have become accustomed to eating it raw. The crisp texture and sweet flavor make it a favorite trail nibble. Nobody else, so far as I know, eats raw Silverweed roots. That is their loss, however. My motto is, "If it tastes good raw, eat it raw."

More commonly, especially for foragers with better memories than I, the starchy roots are boiled for up to twenty minutes before serving. Salt, pepper, and butter complement this vegetable. And despite my preference for raw Silverweed roots, the cooked product is delicious and well worth the effort involved.

Oddly, except for modern foragers, historical reference to coastal residents eating Silverweed is lacking. None of the old-timers of my acquaintance even seems to know what Silverweed is. Here, then, is a "new" plant for today's forager. Enjoy!

Northern Bay
Myrica pensylvanica

Color plate: Figure 8

Use: Spice, flavor additive

Range: Northern Bay is found throughout New England, rarely more than a mile from the coast and often at the water's edge. It prefers infertile soil.

Similarity to toxic species: None

Best time: June through September

Status: Common and abundant

Tools needed: None

Before writing this chapter, I sat down to a hearty ham and lima bean soup, seasoned with Northern Bay leaves. The leaves were picked last summer, dried, and stored in a glass jar in my cupboard. Now, fortified with the essence of that noble spice, it seems proper to write about it.

Hardly a schoolchild lives who hasn't heard of how the early colonists made candles from bayberry wax. The bay also yielded soap to our early settlers—bay wax saponifies well, making a fine soap. Interestingly, little if anything is recorded in the history books about the culinary aspects of Northern Bay.

Although Northern Bay, a member of the wax myrtle family, rarely grows more than 10 feet tall, certain venerable specimens attain heights of better than 20 feet. The so-called berries (really nutlets rather than berries) are coated with a bluish white, aromatic wax that should not be eaten. Instead, it is the leaves that are valuable. These average between 2 and 3 inches long and are shiny on both sides, especially on the upper surface. In fact, they are so shiny that in order to photograph a bay shrub in full sunlight, it is necessary to use a polarizer to cut the glare. The leaves have a few shallow indentations, or notches, near the end that give a slightly toothed appearance. Also, the leaves are broader at the end than at the base. The overall impression anyone gets upon seeing a Northern Bay shrub for the first time is "dense and bushy."

Sometimes, while walking along the shore, I like to take a handful of Northern Bay leaves, crush them in my hand, and savor the penetrating aroma. This lifts my spirits on those low-pressure days when fog hangs thick and dreary on the New England coast.

The leaves can be picked anytime they're large enough to bother with. A pint or so of the stiff, shiny leaves is easily plucked in a few minutes. Next, the leaves should be placed in a paper or cloth bag for the trip home. Don't use plastic; it could cause the leaves to sweat and lose some of their essential oil—and with it, much of their flavor.

The leaves must be thoroughly dried before storing in a glass jar. My favorite method is to line the bottom of my trusty old brown ash basket with bay leaves and hang it on one of the cut nails driven into the beam that extends across my kitchen ceiling. The main thing, however accomplished, is to slow-dry the leaves in the cool shade. When they are brittle, they are ready to go into permanent storage in the spice closet. Be careful not to break the leaves when filling the storage container.

Dried Northern Bay leaves are used in all manner of soups and stews. I add a few leaves to blue mussels prior to steaming, and even to the water that lobsters will be steamed in. When making pickled mussels or pickled periwinkles, I always insert three or four Northern Bay leaves between the meats and the side of the canning jar. The list of uses is endless and limited only by your imagination. Remember, though, to use the leaves whole and discard them after cooking. The flavor will by then have been transferred from the leaf to the food. The spent leaf is tough and insipid. For that reason, never crumple bay leaves before using.

Northern Bay leaves are not the same as commercially available bay leaves, and they don't taste exactly the same, either. Truthfully, the wild Northern Bay has a far superior flavor to the store-bought product. And if the price of commercial bay leaves were figured to the pound, they would surely end up more expensive than the most precious metals. Northern Bay is free.

Although Northern Bay occurs naturally within earshot of the sea, it can grow almost anywhere it is planted, as long as the ground is poor. In fact, while perusing a garden catalog, I was amused to see Northern Bay plants for sale. These cost about seven bucks per shrub. For those who don't have access to the shore, seven dollars seems a small enough investment to ensure a steady supply of Northern Bay leaves.

Wrinkled Rose
Rosa rugosa

Color plate: Figure 9

Use: Survival food, salad ingredient, nutritious tea

Range: Throughout New England, especially along the immediate seashore

Similarity to toxic species: None

Best time: August and September

Status: Common and abundant

Tools needed: None

Wrinkled Rose flowers vary in color from white to pink to carmine. Each flower has five petals. The compound leaves have wrinkled leaflets, and the stems bristle with stiff hairs and sharp, needlelike thorns. Oftentimes, Wrinkled Rose grows in company with the Pasture or Wild Rose, *R. carolina*. The Wild Rose lacks the bristly hairs on the stem, but it does have thorns. Wild Rose petals are pink.

Here in New England, reminders of our seafaring heritage are never farther than the nearest beach. The *rugosa* rose is one such reminder. These hardy plants literally grow everywhere along the seashore. Soil type, sun, or shade—nothing deters this tenacious Asian immigrant. It is said that the old sea captains, many of whose homes still stand, were the first to carry the seed-laden hips of the Wrinkled Rose home to New England. It is a fact that the old-timers were fascinated with the flora and fauna of foreign lands and that they often carried seeds, plants, and whatnot back to New England. A certain awe strikes me every time I view vast sections of seaside banks literally covered with roses that almost certainly are descendants of those brought here by some long-forgotten seafarer.

The flowers themselves are plebeian, poor and primitive when compared to modern hybrid roses. But such as they are, they have much to offer. What seaside picnic isn't enhanced by a bouquet of such ancient and honorable blooms, picked fresh and stuck in whatever container the sea may have to offer? These unkempt roses of our beaches and seashores may be simple, but they own a certain dignity.

There are mountains of recipes for rose hips and petals. Most of these are lengthy and time-consuming and don't interest me very much. Yet Wrinkled Rose, Pasture Rose, and, indeed, all the roses have some simple, basic uses that everyone should have at least a passing acquaintance with. First in line must be the use of hips as survival food.

Rose hips, so called, are really the fruiting bodies of the rose. These contain lots of small seeds and a fleshy, inner pulp. The skin of rose hips is tough and inedible. Some foragers consider rose hips to be a passable trail nibble; I don't. The hips must be split, the seeds and soft pulp discarded, and the more substantial remaining pulp eaten. But no matter how many times I try, I find the flavor reminiscent of chewing on a vitamin C pill . . . a little too astringent for my taste. As a survival food, however, rose hips can't be equaled, because speaking of vitamin C, these tart fruits are one of the world's most potent sources of the cold-fighting vitamin. So barring a liking for the raw pulp (this is possible, although I cannot imagine it), the hips should be considered a top-notch survival food.

After this, a powerful, vitamin C–laden tea can be made from the fresh or dried hips. Again, the hips should be split and the seeds and inner pulp discarded. Some honey dispels the inherent astringency and the tea, besides being good for you, tastes pretty good, too.

Finally, the petals are edible. Nibble them raw or sprinkle them on salads. Use them as a garnish for meat dishes. Above all, use your imagination.

We might say, "A rose is a rose is a rose," but here in New England there's more to the story.

2

Plants of Fertile Streamsides

Fertile streamsides, also known as the alluvial plain, are places of great richness and diverse plant life. The reason for this wonderful fertility may be illustrated by considering any of the world's great rivers. History students know that the Nile, for instance, during its annual floods, deposits nutrient-rich silt and other matter along its banks, ensuring healthy and bountiful crops for farmers who understand and benefit by this endless cycle. And so it is with our New England streams, brooks, and rivers, albeit on a considerably smaller scale.

Certain plants insist upon this rich, nutrient-laden ground and are rarely found in any other situation. Among these are Ostrich Fern, Stinging Nettles, and Wild Oats. Additionally, several species of dock are usually found here, although they sometimes grow in drier conditions, as long as the ground is fertile.

In early spring the alluvial plain resembles a disaster zone. Signs of the recent snowmelt, with its accompanying high water and floods, are everywhere. Bits of dead grass, carried by the torrents and stuck on tree limbs many feet above the ground, wave forlornly in the gentle breeze. Dead trees, limbs akimbo, perhaps brought from far upstream, make walking difficult. And everywhere is a thin layer of damp, but friable silt, the stuff that nature uses to replenish the soil and sustain and nourish streamside plant life.

As the sun warms the soil, the wild plants awaken, peeping through the streamside litter, beckoning the forager to come and partake. This is surely a good time to be alive and poking around in the New England outdoors. It's a brief season, but a glorious one.

Ostrich Fern
Pteretis pensylvanica

Color plate: Figures 10 and 11

Synonyms: Fiddleheads

Use: Cooked vegetable. Cold, cooked fiddleheads can be added to salads.

Range: Fertile streamsides and other rich, damp ground throughout New England

Similarity to toxic species: Pasture Brakes, or Braken, a smaller fern with a nearly round stipe (stem) and a three-parted triangular blade (leaf), grow along streamsides and on damp woodland ground. Young braken are skinny, lack the deep groove of an Ostrich Fern (although they do have a rudimentary groove), and, when young, are a reddish brown color, as opposed to the emerald green of the Ostrich Fern. Braken fiddleheads are scrawny, with an unfinished look. Braken are suspected of being carcinogenic when consumed in large quantities over an extended period. Also, raw or only slightly cooked braken cause intestinal upsets.

Best time: Early spring. This may vary from northern to southern regions, but Ostrich Fern is usually ready mid- to late April in the south and mid-May in the north. In Aroostook County, Maine, fiddleheads persist until June.

Status: Common and abundant

Tools needed: Ostrich Fern fiddleheads must be picked by hand.

The emerging Ostrich Fern frond is called a fiddlehead. In fact, all ferns go through the fiddlehead stage. The likeness to the curled headstock of a violin, or fiddle, is striking. But from here, things become confusing. New Englanders, being frugal of words, simply call immature Ostrich Fern fronds fiddleheads. Suffice it to say, in New England *fiddleheads* means "Ostrich Fern."

Ostrich Fern fiddleheads . . . oh, what the heck. From here on, I'll simply refer to them as fiddleheads too. Fiddleheads are easy to identify. The stem has a deep groove, deeper than the slight groove on any other fern. It has a shiny, green color and is smooth as glass. The curled part, the actual fiddlehead (the folded, curled embryonic fern), is tightly packed, yet by careful unwinding it is possible to uncurl and get a look at the baby plant. Both sides of the fiddlehead are encased in a thin, papery, brown parchmentlike material. Fiddleheads are best when only an inch or two long, and tightly packed.

"Fiddleheading"—walking the streamsides in early spring in search of fiddleheads—is dear to the hearts of many New England country folk. Although most rural people have largely forsaken foraging as a way of life, many continue to go fiddleheading. And those who, for physical or other reasons, cannot go fiddleheading don't go without their fiddleheads. That's what friends are for—to supply fiddleheads to those who need them. Even city dwellers get in the act; fiddleheads are a regular seasonal offering at health food stores and supermarkets. Some places even stock canned fiddleheads, right along with the canned peas and other, more common fodder. Fiddleheads are a New England staple.

Considerable mystique is attached to fiddleheads and fiddleheading. The locations of prime fiddlehead patches are zealously guarded, although goodness knows why; almost any streamside is dotted with patches of fiddleheads, and practically all the major rivers in New England, especially northern New England, have fiddleheads growing along their banks.

Fiddleheads are best picked when the stem is only an inch or two long and before the fronds begin to unfurl. The technique is simple: Grasp the stem as close to the ground as possible and bend until it snaps.

Here are a few tips for the novice fiddlehead picker. First, pay close attention to the temperature. As soon as the ground has thawed and the first few blackflies (biting gnats, the bane of early-spring foragers) appear, it is time to check the fiddlehead patch. Fiddleheads, like some mushrooms, erupt practically overnight. So if the fiddleheads are not quite up yet, wait a few days and check again.

Next, don't neglect the hard-to-reach spots. Paw through the mats of dead grass and pay special attention to the south side of old half-rotten logs. Sometimes the biggest and best fiddleheads are hidden in such spots.

What if someone else has already visited the fiddlehead patch? Don't despair. The root crowns produce multiple fronds over an extended period. They just keep coming. Regarding this, old-time fiddleheaders insist that it weakens the plant to pick all the fiddleheads from a clump; it is prudent to leave at least one remaining. Whether or not this helps the resource, it certainly is a nice way to view things. No matter what plant we are harvesting, we should never take it all.

The papery, brown parchmentlike material that clings to either side of the fiddlehead is easily removed in the woods. Some people, though, leave it on and attempt to wash it off when they get home. Unfortunately, wetting the stuff makes it stick like glue, rendering it very difficult to remove.

Taking this one step farther, it is easiest to remove the brown parchment before the fiddlehead is picked. Either pull the stuff off or tweak the fiddlehead with a forefinger. If some parchment remains after the fiddlehead is picked, tap the fiddlehead to dislodge it. But above all, remove the brown stuff before rinsing the fiddleheads. Any remaining parchment can easily be removed at home.

Fresh, boiled fiddleheads are a springtime staple. For some, the first fiddleheads must be eaten with the first mess of brook trout; the two go naturally together. But the trout are a luxury, not a necessity. The basic fiddlehead recipe is simplicity itself. Boil water in a medium saucepan and add the fresh fiddleheads. Boil until the fiddleheads droop when picked up with a fork, and quickly remove from the water lest the fiddleheads become too soft. Serve with butter and (in this case, it is traditional) a liberal sprinkling of cider vinegar.

If any fiddleheads remain, they can be cooled in the refrigerator and used either alone or with other ingredients in a salad. *Never*, despite what others may say, use raw fiddleheads in a salad; they have a profound laxative effect.

Fiddleheads can also be deep-fried, in the manner of clams or scallops. Dip the raw fiddleheads in a batter, immerse in hot oil, and drain. They're yummy.

Once, a diner in Belfast, Maine, featured fiddlehead quiche on its menu. It being against my better judgment to pay for what is free for the taking, I was unwilling to try this novel dish. The owner, though, put me on the spot, and it was a good thing she did. Her fiddlehead quiche was a treat fit for the gods.

The next is one of my favorite fiddlehead recipes. Boil the fiddleheads according to the standard method and drain them thoroughly. Next, line the bottom of a greased, ovenproof baking dish with a thin layer of the cooked fiddleheads. Now drizzle any kind of cheese sauce (my favorite is Alfredo) on the fiddleheads. Repeat the process by layering fiddleheads and cheese sauce until either the dish is full or the fiddleheads are used up. Finally, sprinkle bread crumbs (I make my own seasoned bread crumbs with day-old bread that I save in a sealed Mason jar, along with my own dried thyme, basil, and oregano) on the top layer of cheese and bake at 350 degrees for thirty minutes or until the top is slightly browned. The finished product is a unique, delicious main-dish meal.

Fiddleheads are one of my wintertime staples. They keep for more than a year in the freezer, with no appreciable loss of flavor or change in texture. I find it easy to store my dozens of bags of fiddleheads by placing the individual bags in plastic, sixteen-ounce margarine tubs before freezing. Two bags easily fit in one tub. The tubs afford additional protection for the produce and stack neatly.

Stinging Nettles
Urtica dioica

Color plate: Figure 12

Use: Cooked vegetable, soup

Range: All through New England on fertile, rich soil, particularly along fertile streamsides

Similarity to toxic species: None

Best time: Late April through late May

Status: Common and abundant

Tools needed: Leather or thick rubber gloves

Most of us, at one time or another, have accidentally brushed against Stinging Nettles. The resulting sting is as sharp and unpleasant as any bee sting. That's because nettle spines contain formic acid, the same stuff many venomous insects carry. Nettle stings, however painful, don't last long and are soon forgotten. Some people consider the occasional nettle sting (the same is often said regarding honeybee stings) to have a prophylactic effect upon the pain of arthritis.

Nettles are an early-spring plant and can usually be found about the same time that Ostrich Fern fiddleheads are ready for picking, and often in the same location. A few years ago a local photographer who specializes in plants asked me to take her to one of my favorite fiddlehead locations so she could take some close-up shots for a magazine. As she was zooming in on a clump of fiddleheads, she casually asked if I knew where she might find some Stinging Nettles. At that very moment my wrist brushed against a nettle plant. With gritted teeth, because of the burning pain, I said, simply, "yes." I hadn't noticed nettles along that particular section of stream before.

It is the young nettle shoots that are eaten. These spring from a labyrinth of buried rhizomes. Each spring the rhizomes push up a new crop of Stinging Nettles. And it is the young shoots only that are good. Mature nettle plants are tough and full of grit.

Nettles have slender flower clusters that sprout from the leaf axils. Recognizing the flowers is but little help for the forager, however, except to mark the spot for the following spring. By the time nettles flower, they are gone by, too far advanced in size for eating. It is better to learn to recognize the immature nettles by the leaves. This is easy because the leaves are generally of a slender, oval shape, are sharply pointed at the tip, and have unusually long petioles, or stems. Further, the leaves grow opposite each other and have well-defined sharp teeth. The upper and lower parts of the leaves, as well as the stem, is covered with fine, hairy bristles, from which comes the sting. Overall, the young plants (best picked when less than 12 inches tall) have a wilted, drooping appearance.

Wear good, protective gloves when picking nettles. It is best to wear long sleeves or, better yet, a sturdy denim jacket to protect wrists and arms. The young nettles are best when snapped or broken near the base of the stem. Sometimes, especially in soft, deep soil, the entire shoot will be dislodged and pull free from the ground. If that happens, don't worry. The underground rhizomes will soon send forth another shoot.

Place the nettles, tender stem, leaves, and tops in a pail, basket, or canvas bag. At home, still wearing gloves, spread the nettles on a tabletop to search for any foreign matter: sticks, grasses, and so on. Next, the nettles can be chopped with a knife or shears. After washing, the nettles can be cooked immediately or refrigerated for a day or so.

Boiled nettles may sound homely and plain, but no better vegetable can be found in the wild or in the supermarket. In a medium saucepan, add a scant bit of water—just enough to cover the bottom. Rinse the nettles but don't drain them. Turn on the heat, and as soon as the water bubbles, add the nettles. Cover, reduce the heat to low, and simmer for fifteen or twenty minutes.

Next, lift the nettles from the pot, allowing them to drain back into the cooking liquid. Do not discard the liquid. It will be used later as a soup. Serve the nettles with a pat of butter, salt, and pepper. A more palatable, wholesome vegetable cannot be found.

The juice, which by now has turned a dark green, is the base for a unique soup. Save the soup for another time, or serve it separately with the cooked nettles. Either way, to the nettle broth, add salt, pepper, and a splash of cider vinegar. Let the mixture simmer before serving in small soup bowls.

Last summer it occurred to me that the nettle broth might be as good cold as hot. One unusually warm and humid afternoon, I added the salt, pepper, and vinegar to some nettle juice from the previous day. I can't remember what my main course was for that lunch, but the cold nettle soup impressed me. It was surprisingly pleasant and tasty.

A more complex nettle soup is made by combining chicken stock or canned broth with nettle leaves, a cut-up onion, a pat of butter, and salt and pepper. Let the mixture simmer until the onion is cooked through. In Scotland a bit of heavy cream is added to the nettle soup before serving. It's hearty, satisfying fare, this Scottish soup.

Incidentally, for those who wonder about such things, nettles lose their stinging properties when cooked.

Curled Dock
Rumex crispus (also other *Rumex* species)

Color plate: Figures 13 and 14

Use: Cooked, green vegetable

Range: Throughout New England along fertile streamsides, in rich fields, and on damp roadsides

Similarity to toxic species: None. All the dock varieties are edible.

Best time: Late April through early June

Status: Common and abundant. A hardy weed.

Tools needed: None

During the dark days of the Great Depression, my family enjoyed an eclectic diet, eating such things as roasted young woodchuck, smoked white suckers, sucker roe, and Curled Dock. Later, because these things reminded them of the hard times, they avoided them. It wasn't until late in his life that my grandpa told me about dock. "It's like spinach," he said, without much enthusiasm. It happened that this was in early May, when the dock was at its peak. I went out that afternoon, picked a bunch of tender young dock leaves, brought them home, and steamed them. They did taste something like spinach, but had a better flavor.

Many years after my initial experience with dock, I went on a weeklong camping and fishing trip in northern Maine. Vowing to live off the land for a week, I brought no food except salt, pepper, and butter. The trout cooperated, providing the meat part of my diet. Then there was the dock. The big, mixed-growth northern forest is perhaps the most difficult place for a forager to find sufficient provender. Since this was June, even the cut-over areas offered but scant fare, the raspberries being not quite ripe and the blueberries still at the tiny, hard green stage. Had it not been for the ubiquitous dock, my trip would probably have been cut short. By the week's end, it became difficult to swallow another forkful of trout, but I still enjoyed the dock.

Dock, which is a member of the buckwheat family, is often said to be a bitter herb, fit to eat only after being boiled in three changes of water. This may be true in late summer, when the curly leaves become tough and unpalatable. But in season, which can be as early as April in southern New England and as late as early June in northern Maine, dock is a superior vegetable, sweet and mild.

Dock, when growing in the open, can attain heights of up to 4 feet, but most plants are between 1 and 2 feet tall. The individual leaves, which are picked and eaten, are up to 10 inches long, thin, and have wavy edges, hence the name Curled Dock. A papery, moist membrane surrounds the petiole, or leafstalk, where it attaches to the stem. The seed stalk is covered with chestnut brown, winged seeds in fall. These are popular in dried flower arrangements. It is possible to dry these seeds, thresh them, and grind them into a flour substitute, but the effort involved is (for me, at least) too great in comparison to the end result.

Another dock, Broad or Red-Veined Dock, has wide, heart-shaped leaves. This dock is best gathered in early spring because it becomes bitter later in the summer. Broad dock often grows in the beds of seasonal streams and is one of the earliest greens to be found in spring, often presenting itself when patches of snow still cling to the north-facing slopes.

Cook either dock as you would spinach. Place the fresh leaves in boiling water and cook until tender. Dock retains most of its bulk in cooking, with the cooked product occupying about as much space as the raw material. Drain immediately after cooking and season with butter, salt, and pepper. Dock is enhanced by a splash of cider vinegar, but this isn't necessary.

Folklore about dock is mostly concerned with its curative powers regarding Stinging Nettle rash. Country children seem to know intuitively to rub crushed dock leaves on nettle stings. Even children whose parents know nothing about dock or nettles use dock. My guess is that ongoing generations of children hand this knowledge down without the slightest need of adult intercession.

Dock, besides tasting as good or better than any similar cultivated leafy vegetable, is a veritable powerhouse of vitamins, particularly vitamins A and C. Dock is also a significant source of protein. Want to go on a health food regimen? Incorporate dock into your diet. Fresh trout helps, too.

Wild Oats
Uvularia sessilifolia

Color plate: Figure 15

Synonyms: Sessile Bellwort

Use: Cooked vegetable, salad ingredient, trail nibble

Range: Throughout New England along streamsides and in damp, rich woodlands

Similarity to toxic species: None

Best time: April and May

Status: Locally abundant

Tools needed: None

One particular day along Maine's Kennebec River stands out in my mind for two reasons. First, red quill mayflies hatched in profuse quantities, and huge brown trout noisily slurped them in. And second, the fertile plain along the river was covered with Ostrich Fern fiddleheads, mingled with dense patches of Wild Oats. All of these pleasing items in one place, at one time, made a big impression on me.

Wild Oats, actually a member of the lily family, sometimes reach a foot in height, but more often are a little more than half that. The forked stems remind me of little, thin chicken wishbones. The leaves are sessile, attached directly to the stem. When in bloom, the bell-shaped (hence the other common name, bellwort) yellow flowers depend from a thin stem.

Wild Oats have never been big on my list of plants to gather in huge quantities and bring home to cook. Although they are plentiful enough, it would make me feel guilty to harvest many of them because they possess, at least to my way of thinking, a certain ethereal quality that would be destroyed by harvesting in quantity. My favorite use is to simply enjoy them fresh by picking the young shoot, stripping all green matter, and nibbling raw. One or two shoots are enough to satisfy my taste and assuage my appetite until more substantial fare can be found.

It doesn't bother me, either, to add a handful of Wild Oats shoots to my gathering basket, especially if enough other plants are around that can be combined to make a wild salad. Oat shoots are a pleasant addition to such a salad. Cooking, though, is the commonly accepted method, and every forager should give cooked Wild Oats a try and take it from there. Boil the tender shoots for at least ten minutes and serve with butter, salt, and pepper.

Don't be swayed by my preference for raw shoots; the cooked vegetable is fine table fare, too, and if lots of Wild Oats are present on your local fertile streamside, by all means go for it. These branched perennial plants are a real symbol of a New England spring in all its finery, and they are there for us to enjoy.

Marsh Marigold
Caltha palustris

Color plate: Figure 16

Synonyms: Cowslip

Use: Cooked vegetable

Range: Throughout New England along slow-moving streams and in swamps

Similarity to toxic species: The flowers are somewhat similar to those of the toxic Common Buttercup. The leaves of the two species are markedly different, however.

Best time: May

Status: Locally abundant

Tools needed: A jackknife helps when cutting individual leaves.

Except that Marsh Marigolds grow in marshes, both common names for this pretty, springtime plant are misleading. Marsh Marigold is not a marigold and is definitely not a cowslip, but instead is closely related to the Common Buttercup. This points out the value of using the scientific name of our favorite plants whenever possible, as opposed to the often misleading common name.

One particular stand of Marsh Marigolds is impressed upon my memory as surely as if it were in a color photograph. These Marsh Marigolds grow in the middle of a little winding stream in the headwaters of a great wetland. When the sun strikes the bright yellow flowers, they shine like beacons. The first time I saw this massive stand of Marsh Marigolds, I instantly thought of William Wordsworth's poem:

> *I wandered lonely as a cloud*
> *That floats on high o'er vales and hills,*
> *When all at once I saw a crowd,*
> *A host of golden daffodils.*

That many daffodils would be hard to find in New England. But the golden Marsh Marigolds make a good substitute.

Marsh Marigolds were another one of my grandparents' Great Depression staples, and as such were not on the table when I came along. They told me about the plants, though, with some degree of fondness.

Marsh Marigolds stand from 6 inches to 2 feet tall. The flowers are bright yellow and resemble Common Buttercup flowers. The dark green leaves, which are the parts that are eaten, are shiny, and heart or kidney shaped. The stem is hollow. The flowers close at night and open during the day.

The time to harvest Marsh Marigold leaves is before and during the time the plant is in blossom. Carefully cut or snap the leaves from the stalk. This will not harm the plant if only a few leaves are taken.

Most people feel the need to cook Marsh Marigold leaves in two or three changes of water, in order to make the plants milder. Also, they contain a sharp-tasting toxin that is rendered harmless by boiling; the different waters remove any trace of the toxin. That said, I cook the leaves in only one water and never detect any strong taste. Also, I have never suffered any ill effects from cooking this way. No matter how many waters are used, however, do this: Get the water boiling first. Thoroughly wash the leaves and immerse them in the boiling water. Leave the leaves in for at least twenty minutes, drain the leaves, and discard the water.

Marsh Marigold leaves are prime when Ostrich Fern fiddleheads, dock, Stinging Nettles, and Wild Oats are ready, and it's not unusual for all these plants to be found in the same location. One caveat: Springtime in New England means bugs, both mosquitoes and, in the northern climes, blackflies. Insect repellent containing deet will keep the bugs from biting. Make sure to get the bug dope on your wrists, the back of your neck, and around pant cuffs and sock tops. Wash the repellent off at the end of the day. Some people are afraid of the chemicals in bug repellents and wear a headnet instead. Headnets drive me to distraction, though, because they are so hard to see through.

3

Plants of Disturbed and Cultivated Ground

The next time the highway department grades a nearby roadside ditch, take note. That now-barren ground will, in a short time, be covered with a variety of interesting, and useful, wild plants. Seeds, brought in on the wind, deposited by birds, or perhaps already present in the ground, dormant and waiting for the grader blade to stir them to life, will germinate, and a rush of green growth will magically transform the formerly lifeless roadside into a carpet of green.

Then there is the cultivated ground, perhaps our own flower or vegetable gardens or the local farmer's cornfield, where "weeds" vex and thwart all but the most determined efforts to eradicate them. Sadly, many of the plants that people strive to conquer are nutritionally superior to the cultivated plants that displace them.

The basic premise behind disturbed and cultivated ground is that nature will not permit it to remain barren for long. And ironically, the act of cultivating, grading, or scraping is what makes this ground suitable for so many useful plants. Our efforts to make letter-perfect garden beds only encourage the invading weeds. Perhaps it's time we foragers recognize that the wild plants have a legitimate right to grow alongside our cabbage and tomatoes. Take a tip from me and consider the vegetable plot a multiuse area, home to both cultivated plants and their valuable wild cousins.

Lamb's-Quarters
Chenopodium album

Color plate: Figures 17 and 18

Synonyms: Pigweed

Use: Cooked vegetable, attractor plant for leaf miners

Range: Cultivated and recently disturbed ground throughout New England

Similarity to toxic species: Mexican tea, *C. ambrosioides,* is a smelly look-alike. The difference is easily determined because the Mexican tea leaves smell like varnish.

Best time: May and throughout the growing season

Status: Common, despised as a difficult-to-eradicate weed

Tools needed: None

Lamb's-Quarters, another member of the goosefoot family, are easily identified. Mature plants can grow to a height of 3 feet. The spear-shaped leaves have wide, uneven teeth and are covered with a grainy, white substance. If in doubt, rub the leaf with a finger; the white powder will feel rough and coarse. In late summer tiny black seeds by the thousands are formed on the flower stem, which grows in the leaf axils.

By the time grass needs the first mowing of the season, it is time to thin the Lamb's-Quarters in my vegetable garden. This is an eagerly anticipated event on my gardening calendar. The diminutive Lamb's-Quarters grow overly thick and must be thinned. At the same time, the 3- to 5-inch plants provide the first meal of Lamb's-Quarters for the season. The incongruity of thinning Lamb's-Quarters is, of course, that at the same time other gardeners are *weeding* their garden beds, ripping up all the Lamb's-Quarters and throwing them on the ground to wither and dry. How often we disparage the best of the best, through lack of knowledge. It's a pity.

The best areas of the garden to encourage Lamb's-Quarters are where the late-season crops, such as winter squash, are planted. These tender plants cannot stand much cold, and seeds or seedlings fail if planted while the soil temperature is much less than seventy degrees. The result is that these particular garden beds are vacant in spring, while other beds are active. Instead of planting quick-growing spring crops like radishes or lettuce, I allow the Lamb's-Quarters to do their thing, thinning the crop as needed for the table.

Here's a practical tip for thinning Lamb's-Quarters and any similar vegetables: Don't pull the plant up by the roots. This creates extra work, because the roots have to be removed later, a tedious task. Better to use kitchen shears and snip the tender plants near the ground. This makes cleaning the harvest easier—and at the same time, the intact roots help improve the tilth, or friability, of the soil.

When the Lamb's-Quarters are about a foot high, the time is right to harvest a great quantity. Most of the plant, except for the thickest part of the stem, can be taken. You can either steam or boil Lamb's-Quarters, just as you would Orache (see page 5). By now, having eaten Lamb's-Quarters three or four times already, the appetite for these delightful greens is partially assuaged and it is time to freeze the surplus. These blanch quickly, after which they are chilled in ice-cold water, drained, put into pint freezer bags, and lovingly placed in the freezer. Lamb's-Quarters freeze well, lasting up to a year in the freezer without any discernible change in taste or texture.

About those Lamb's-Quarter plants in the winter squash bed. Rather than harvest all of the plants, it is my practice to leave one or two of the biggest, lushest specimens to grow to maturity. This kills two birds with one proverbial stone. First, it guarantees a crop of Lamb's-Quarter seeds and an ongoing supply of Lamb's-Quarters. And second, the fully grown plants act as an attractor for leaf miners, those maddening little pests that leave ugly "snail trails" on the leaves of cultivated plants as they burrow through the leaf. Leaf miners love to work their way through Lamb's-Quarter leaves; the bigger and thicker the Lamb's-Quarter plant, the better the cussed bugs like them. I'm convinced that leaf miner damage to my cultivated crops is lessened considerably because of the presence of the Lamb's-Quarters.

But that's not all. After the leaf miners have had their fling, the Lamb's-Quarters continue to sprout new branchlets and leaves. It helps to do some light pruning throughout the season on these plants to encourage new growth. By fall, just before the big killing frosts reduce all tender vegetation to blackened, withered crisps, the last picking of Lamb's-Quarters can take place.

From the lengths I go to for Lamb's-Quarters, you've doubtless guessed that I think the plants are worth the effort. This is one of the most tender and sweet vegetables available, including all of the cultivated varieties. With this in mind, what about those who don't have garden beds and no place to encourage Lamb's-Quarters? Don't despair. Go to a spot where the ground was disturbed the previous year, perhaps a vacant lot or some such place. Lamb's-Quarters are efficient pioneers and are able to take advantage of ripe ground at a moment's notice. For those living in the country, head to the nearest farm and ask the farmer for permission to pick some "weeds" from the edge of his manure pile. Lamb's-Quarters don't like fresh manure, but thrive on the ancient rotted stuff, such as is found behind and around the edges of manure piles.

It wouldn't be fitting to end this chapter with talk of foraging around old manure piles. Lamb's-Quarters are a noble plant and deserve better. If this plant ever achieves the recognition that is its due, Lamb's-Quarters will be sold in supermarkets and health food stores at outrageous prices. People will scour the countryside looking for stands of Lamb's-Quarters. But until that happens, we foragers have unlimited access to one of the most tasty and nutritious plants in the world. And for us, it is free. Perhaps we should keep it our secret for just a little longer.

Quickweed
Galinsoga ciliata (also *G. parviflora* where available)

Color plate: Figure 19

Synonyms: Galinsoga

Use: Cooked vegetable

Range: Throughout New England

Similarity to toxic species: None

Best time: July through September

Status: A despised weed and widely abundant

Tools needed: None

Quickweed, a member of the daisy family, grows on recently disturbed ground. Quickweed, or galinsoga, as some call it, is not an old-time favorite of New England foragers, nor does it have much of a history in the region. It is a relatively new plant, having crept in from the Deep South and Mexico, and many otherwise knowledgeable foragers have yet to discover it. That's their loss, though. It is good stuff.

In fact, my first encounter with Quickweed came as a result of a load of composted cow manure being delivered to my garden. The stuff was laden with Quickweed, which immediately took over several of my garden beds. The first year's crop of Quickweed was wasted because I didn't know it was good eating. I ruthlessly pulled each plant (an easy job—it's shallow rooted) from the garden, hoping to get rid of this strange invader once and for all. Failing that, I determined to learn more about this noxious intruder. My sleuthing paid off. I found out that Quickweed is edible! I allowed the tiny plants that remained to grow to usable size, picked them, boiled them for a little less than ten minutes, and sat at the table for my first taste of Quickweed.

Hindsight, it is said, is valueless. In my case, it was less than valueless. The stuff I had worked so hard to eradicate was better in all respects than most of my cultivated vegetables. *Chagrin* barely describes my emotions. . . . I had discarded a season's supply of one of the better greens in the garden. But it wouldn't happen again.

Quickweed is identified by its ovate, roughly toothed leaves, hairy stem (at least with *G. ciliata*), and unfinished-looking flower. The flower resembles a miniature daisy, with half the petals removed at equal intervals, leaving a tiny yellow disc and four tiny groups of petals at the four compass points.

Pick a good mess of Quickweed for the first try . . . it loses some bulk in cooking. My favorite way is to boil it for about ten minutes, drain, and serve with real butter and a bit of salt. Vinegar complements Quickweed, but that is a matter of taste. I like the flavor of the plant well enough that for me it doesn't need any imparted extra flavor.

This inconspicuous, lowly invader from the warmer climes may be hated by most, but those of us who know its virtues praise it.

Field Peppergrass
Lepidium campestre

Color plate: Figure 20

Synonyms: Cow Cress

Use: Trail nibble, salad ingredient, cooked vegetable

Range: Throughout New England

Similarity to toxic species: None

Best time: May and June, but new growth continues all summer, especially after the first frost

Status: An alien weed, despised by most. Common and abundant.

Tools needed: None

Like so many of my favorite wild vegetables, peppergrass came to my garden via a truckload of composted cow manure. The compost had lain, uncovered, for some time before being sold, and seeds of various "weeds" had sufficient time to take hold. The four petals on the little yellow flowers told me immediately that here was one of the mustards. Now, instead of driving hither and yon to get the occasional supply of peppergrass, my own personal supply was solidly established. The farmer didn't realize the good deal he had given me.

Another member of the *Lepidium* genus, Poor-Man's-Pepper (*L. virginicum,* which has stalked leaves), is equally as good as Field Peppergrass, and the two can be used interchangeably. And speaking of related plants, the *young* leaves of Common Horseradish *(Armoracia lapathifolia)* can be used the same as peppergrass. This was news to me when, a few years ago, an old-timer asked my opinion of boiled horseradish leaves. He told me that when he was young, his parents regularly served boiled horseradish leaves while they were in season. Having never tried them, I had no opinion. That changed after my first taste of the spicy greens. They added much-appreciated zest to my noontime meal.

As with so many other wild plants, my all-time favorite use of Field

Peppergrass is as a casual nibble. It is my habit, when passing Field Peppergrass, to pick a few tender tips and leaves and chew on them without giving the act much thought. But they also make a superb ingredient to impromptu salads and are a tasty vegetable when boiled for around ten minutes.

Learn to recognize Field Peppergrass by its dark green, slender, deeply toothed leaves, which are attached directly to the stem of the plant, and by the thin flower spikes with their small, four-petaled yellow flowers. Once this tentative identification is made, it is safe to take a small nibble. The pungent mustard flavor, while not strong or offensive, is immediately evident.

Green Amaranth
Amaranthus retroflexus

Color plate: Figure 21

Synonyms: Amaranth, Pigweed

Use: Cooked vegetable

Range: Throughout New England

Similarity to toxic species: None

Best time: From the time it is big enough to pick, usually May, until the plant is killed by frost

Status: Uncontrollable weed, common and abundant

Tools needed: None

Amaranth is an aggressive transplant from the South, and is believed to have been among the earliest plants cultivated by North American Indians. It does best on cultivated ground; commercial fields that are plowed and harrowed each year are a favorite location. One place stands out in my mind—a massive cornfield filled with silage corn for use as dairy cow feed. The corn was harvested and chopped, leaving a field half filled with 2-foot amaranth plants. The leaves from the amaranth in this field could have fed all the inhabitants of the town for a month, three times daily. But the inevitable happened: The farmer plowed this valuable, green vegetable back into the ground, along with the corn stubble. This scenario is reenacted many thousands of times each year across the United States and southern Canada.

Green Amaranth is easy to identify. The leaves are the most important feature. They have blunt ends, are wider at the base than at the tip, and have a prominent center rib, with alternate veins issuing from the midrib. They are dark green on top, but have a gauzy, reddish hue on the bottom. The seed spikes, which appear late in the summer, are somewhat prickly.

Amaranth is, to my taste, a palatable, albeit somewhat mild, spinach substitute. Once, I diligently tended my spinach crop. In order to give the spinach every opportunity, I pulled out all the amaranth, the primary weed, in the spinach bed. Even so, the spinach was slow growing, and when it finally achieved a useful size, it bolted. After the spinach was long gone, amaranth continued to grow and I ate it all season long. It was as good as the spinach I had wasted so much time on.

Eventually, wisdom prevailed. I realized that it was impractical to raise spinach when amaranth was so abundant. I don't grow spinach anymore.

Pick the leaves and tender tips any time the plant is large enough, throughout the season. Boil for fifteen or twenty minutes. Amaranth loses some bulk in cooking, but not as much as Lamb's-Quarters. Drain thoroughly and serve with butter, salt, pepper, and a splash of cider vinegar. Amaranth keeps well in the freezer.

Purslane
Portulaca oleracea

Color plate: Figure 22

Synonyms: Pusley

Use: Cooked vegetable, salad ingredient

Range: Throughout the area, in cultivated soil

Similarity to toxic species: None

Best time: June through September

Status: Abundant weed

Tools needed: None

It has taken me a lifetime to say "Purslane" instead of "pusley," the latter being the old-time name that my grandpa used for this ubiquitous, vining plant. Purslane is universally despised by gardeners because once it appears, it cannot be eradicated. That said, I'm glad purslane found its way to my vegetable garden. Now I don't have to rely upon others for my supply of this prized vegetable.

To paraphrase an old saw, "Purslane not only tastes good, it's good for you." It was probably introduced to this country by design rather than accident. Highly esteemed around the world, Purslane has medicinal as well as culinary uses. First, the sticky juice from the crushed stems and leaves can be used in much the same way aloe juice is used, for relief from stings, burns, and bites. Other health benefits may be reaped by eating the cooked vegetable: It is rich in vitamins C and A, as well as the beneficial omega-3 acids. Oh, yes, Purslane also contains good amounts of calcium and phosphorus. It's a regular, natural vitamin pill.

Before Purslane invaded my vegetable garden, I decided to try raising the cultivated variety, something euphemistically called Golden Purslane. As might be expected, the Golden Purslane didn't stack up to its wild cousin. The germination rate was poor; the stuff didn't have the sprawling habit of wild Purslane, either, and thus didn't offer a sufficient quantity for a big Purslane eater like me. And insects attacked it with a vengeance, something that rarely happens to wild Purslane. This was my second attempt to grow a cultivated type of a wild plant, and like the first attempt it was a failure. It's so hard to improve on something that is pretty near perfect in the first place.

Purslane is readily identified by its dark green, paddle-shaped leaves, each from approximately $1/2$ to $3/4$ inch long. These leaves are not green on the bottom, however. Instead, they have a whitish sheen that sparkles in the sun, something like moonlight reflecting off freshly fallen snow. Purslane has insignificant yellow five-petaled flowers.

Rarely does Purslane rise more than 1 inch above the ground. Rather, the thick, reddish, succulent stem branches and spreads, like different divisions of an invading host, making simultaneous flank, rear, and frontal attacks on an unsuspecting enemy.

Purslane stems can be snipped indiscriminately; new growth will soon follow. Take the ends of the stems, the most tender part. I use a colander instead of a basket for gathering. That way, it is easy to take the Purslane inside and rinse. Rinsing should be thorough, because the stems can pick up grit from the soil. After the vegetable is thoroughly clean, chop it into inch-long sections. There's no need to strip the leaves.

Next, the cleaned, chopped Purslane has several uses. It can be boiled or steamed for about ten minutes, drained, and served as a green vegetable with the usual butter, salt, and pepper. But my favorite use is in stir-fries. Purslane can be the sole ingredient, or one of many, in a delightful wild stir-fry.

For the first Purslane stir-fry of the season, I don't add other ingredients; I want to fully appreciate this tender, sweet vegetable. I use a good, low-sodium soy sauce and make my own hot mustard by mixing powdered English mustard with water and perhaps a drop of white vinegar. The Purslane is stir-fried until it is limp and served with a side dish of rice. A cheap meal, but one as nutritious and savory as all get out.

Purslane keeps for a long time in the crisper drawer of the refrigerator. If it gets a bit limp, soak it in cold water for five minutes, drain, and it is ready for use.

Lady's Thumb
Polygonum persicaria

Color plate: Figure 23

Synonyms: Redleg

Use: Cooked vegetable

Range: In waste places throughout the area, particularly damp areas

Similarity to toxic species: None

Best time: May through September

Status: Widespread and common

Tools needed: None

Lady's Thumb, another member of the widespread buckwheat family, is one of those plants that everybody sees but few take time to identify. For years, I didn't know what it was, referring to it in my mind as "that droopy-looking weed that grows across the street by the henhouse." Then, when it appeared near my place, I decided it was time to learn more about it. The Lady's Thumb turned out to be a delicious boiling green, which came as no surprise considering its relationship to another eminently edible plant, Japanese Knotweed. To my knowledge, Lady's Thumb has never been and is not currently a popular wild food in New England. I'm the only person I know who eats it. And maybe now you.

Lady's Thumb has several identifying features. First, the dark blotch on the upper part of each leaf is its trademark, the so-called Lady's Thumb print. The leaves are lance shaped, with no discernible teeth. The leaf margins, however, are quite wavy. Where the leaves join the stem, they are covered by a membranous sheath, similar to the sheath on the joints of Japanese Knotweed. The tiny pinkish white flowers are borne on short spikes. Finally, the plant has an overall wilted appearance, as if the hot, noonday sun was too much for it.

Lady's Thumb is said to acquire a bit of an acrid taste in summer. I've never noticed this. The Lady's Thumb on my land seems as sweet and mild as the most tender young spinach. But since it is one of the smartweeds, and the word *smartweed* presumably refers to a peppery quality when eaten, it is possible that Lady's Thumb differs from place to place, which is not at all unusual.

My main problem with Lady's Thumb is there is not enough of it around my place to give me more than a few meals a summer. And although it would be easy enough for me to go elsewhere and gather an abundant supply, I am content to husband the local crop and appreciate what it gives me. Some things are enhanced in value if they are dear. Lady's Thumb is like that.

Pick only the leaves. Wash them, drain them, and drop them whole in a slight amount of boiling water. Cook for no longer than ten minutes, or until the leaves turn color and become limp. Drain and serve. Lady's Thumb responds well to a few drops of cider vinegar. Salt and pepper are optional. Lady's Thumb leaves lose bulk when cooking, so use a bit more of the raw product than seems necessary and the proportions should work out.

— 4 —
Woodland Plants of the Mottled Shade

Old-growth forests, the kind with a dense canopy, offer little in the way of wild foods. That's also true of plantations of Red Pine, and of the fir "jungles" of northern New England. They're simply not likely places for the forager. That's because the plants that we seek need some measure of sun, and sun cannot penetrate a thick forest canopy.

Some of the edible wildlings, though, cannot live in direct sun either. They require mottled or dappled shade—a mixture of sun and shade. For the most part, these plants live in the rich loam in or along the edges of mixed-growth woodlands. Some of the best-tasting and most interesting plants live in the mottled shade of our New England woodlands.

Clintonia
Clintonia borealis

Color plate: Figure 24

Synonyms: Corn Lily

Use: Trail nibble, salad ingredient, cooked vegetable

Range: Woodland edges and rich loam throughout New England

Similarity to toxic species: At a certain point in its development, Clintonia vaguely resembles Lily-of-the-Valley. If the broken leaf does not smell like cucumbers, avoid the plant.

Best time: May

Status: Common locally

Tools needed: A jackknife or kitchen shears helps trim the young leaves.

Clintonia's appearance belies its taste. Who would think that this pretty spring wildflower, with its shiny green leaves, would taste exactly like a cucumber? This cucumber taste is convenient for people like me who hate to buy anything they can easily grow themselves, in this case, cucumbers. When cukes are not in season, the craving for them intensifies and Clintonia fills the void. While Clintonia lacks any resemblance to a cucumber in texture or appearance, the fresh, chopped leaf adds an authentic and unmistakable cucumber taste to any salad. The leaves can also be boiled or steamed.

As with so many wild vegetables, Clintonia must be gathered at or before one particular stage of its development, in this case before the leaves completely unfurl. Past this stage the pleasant cucumber flavor becomes rank and overpowering. Clintonia is the Jekyll and Hyde of the plant world, with both a delightful and an unpleasant side.

Here is a comparison that will help identify the young Clintonia leaves: they look for all the world like starched green napkins, neatly wrapped and standing at stiff attention at the dinner table. In June the warmer days will cause the leaves to unfurl and assume a totally different appearance. The adult plant has basal leaves that are about 6 inches long, are shiny and smooth, and have a prominent midvein. The nodding yellow flowers are delicate and are borne atop a naked stalk. In midsummer the fruit, or berries, are dark blue.

Clintonia is usable for only a few short weeks out of the year. This ephemeral quality adds to the allure of this attractive and good-tasting woodland lily.

Indian Cucumber
Medeola virginica

Color plate: Figures 25 and 26

Use: Trail nibble

Range: Shaded woods throughout New England

Similarity to toxic species: None

Best time: June through August

Status: Locally abundant, but scarce in some areas. Dig roots only from large colonies.

Tools needed: Indian cucumber root can be extracted by hand, but a long, narrow hand trowel is a help.

Common plant names are, more often than not, misleading and confusing. Here we have a woodland plant, Indian Cucumber, that tastes not the least bit like a cucumber and another woodland plant, Clintonia, or Corn Lily, that tastes exactly like a cucumber, but is named for corn, which it definitely does not taste like. It's a conundrum.

Indian Cucumber is, without question, the best raw wild edible going. The taste (which, as I previously mentioned, is nothing like a cucumber) is sweet, mild, and a little nutty. The crisp texture of an Indian Cucumber reminds me of an Icicle Radish. Because of its long season, availability, wide range, and exquisite flavor, Indian Cucumber is a favorite of hikers and backpackers. Here is a plant that lots of people know about and everybody loves.

Notice that Indian Cucumber is listed solely as a trail nibble. It is possible to pickle the roots, but to pick that many seems greedy to me. It is better to regard Indian Cucumber simply as a trail snack, a special treat when encountered by chance. Digging kills the plant, although any roots left in the ground will grow another plant. Appreciate the root of this delicious plant for what it is: a wonderfully pleasant gift of nature.

That said, it might be wondered how a hiker or forager could dare eat any root raw, straight from the ground. Is it sanitary? Probably it is best to dig the roots where found and thoroughly wash them before eating, even if that involves going to some lengths. That's not how I do it, though, and here's my rationale. Indian Cucumber grows only in good, rich, woodland soil. As long as nothing dangerous or nasty is found nearby, it should be perfectly fine to dig the root, wipe off all loose soil, and eat the thing as is. What would be dangerous, however, is to eat any raw vegetable from the average organic garden; such soil is rich in manure. And, non-organic garden soil may contain various toxic chemicals. Pure, woodland soil generally does not present such hazards. But do as I say, not as I do, and wash your Indian Cucumber roots, for safety's sake.

The digging may be done with a trowel, but it must not be done carelessly or willy-nilly. That's because the root lies horizontally in the ground, not vertically; in other words, it is at right angles to the stem. Because of this habit, it is impossible to know, without probing with the fingers, which direction the root points. So gently probe the soil at the base of the stem first, then grab the large end of the root and, while applying gentle, steady pressure, slowly work it back and forth until it breaks free. This may be likened to picking up nightcrawlers, those big earthworms that come out on wet nights; the worm will break if pulled roughly and quickly, but if steady, even pressure is applied, the worm soon relinquishes its grip on the sides of its burrow and pulls free easily. This same technique is useful in pulling carrots and parsnips. Easy does it is the key.

Indian Cucumber has a singular appearance, with anywhere from five to seven or more basal leaves arranged in a whorl and a group of three to five smaller leaves atop a long, thin stem. The basal leaves are relatively slender and pointed, while the leaves atop the stem are a bit fatter; they resemble the leaves of another woodland plant, the bunchberry. The drooping yellow flowers are insignificant. These later develop into inedible blue berries.

The stem, which can grow nearly 3 feet long, is covered with a white fuzz that can be twisted between the fingers like lint, or gathered in a bunch and slid up or down the stem.

The roots, or rhizomes, are about 2 inches long when mature, wide at the stem end and thinly tapered at the extreme end. They have small, hairlike rootlets here and there. These rootlets ought to be rubbed off before eating.

Large-Leafed Aster
Aster macrophyllus

Color plate: Figures 27 and 28

Use: Cooked vegetable

Range: Throughout New England

Similarity to toxic species: None

Best time: May

Status: Common and abundant, in dense colonies

Tools needed: None

Sometime in May, depending upon what part of New England you're in, the Large-Leafed Asters are ready for picking. A good rule of thumb is to seek the asters when the woodpeckers drum. Part of a woodpecker courtship ritual (various types of woodpeckers engage in this same ritual, by the way) is for the male to drum on some object that resonates loudly—usually a dead tree, but metal trash cans, aluminum boats, and even the sides of buildings are sometimes used. When the drumming becomes a regular din, when the woodlands echo with the hammering of multiple woodpeckers, all vying with each other to see who can make the most racket, that's when the Large-Leafed Asters are prime.

A member of the daisy family, Large-Leafed Asters lead a sort of double life. In spring the roughly toothed basal leaves are the only noticeable part of the plant. In late summer the plant sends up a stalk and sets flowers. The flowers range from white to reddish blue. The stalk has some small, sessile leaves. Someone seeing a group of these plants in spring may have difficulty recognizing them in fall, they look so strikingly different.

It helps to recognize Large-Leafed Asters—indeed, any edible plant—at all stages of its development. That way, the plant can be noted at any time of year and visited at just the correct stage for picking.

Large-Leafed Asters, to my knowledge, have absolutely no history as table fare in New England, and it is doubtful that more than a handful of people are aware of their potential as an excellent spring green. But their lack of popularity does not diminish their great taste. They are sweet, mild, and leave no unpleasant aftertaste.

My cottage is located in a woodland setting. The edge of my lawn is the edge of the woods and is full of Large-Leafed Asters. All I need to do is go out with basket in hand and pick a bunch of leaves. This can be done while other components of the meal are cooking, because the leaves cook quickly. When the plants are prime, which is when they are no more than 4 inches long, they are a regular, springtime addition to my table. Later, the leaves become tough and not worth bothering with.

Don't worry about hurting the resource by picking the springtime leaves of Large-Leafed Aster. As long as soil and light conditions are propitious, they will thrive. These asters are tough and durable. Indeed, I once mowed a path through a big bed of Large-Leafed Asters. They quickly grew back and, when mowed a second time, grew back with renewed vigor. This is a hardy plant.

The leaves reduce slightly in bulk when boiled. Get a pot with a little water boiling and drop in a few handfuls of washed Large-Leafed Aster leaves. Cook until the leaves turn color and are limp. Drain and serve with the usual accompaniments. As with so many of these woodland plants, the season is short, so enjoy the Large-Leafed Asters when they are ripe for the picking. They are more than worth what slight effort it takes to pick and cook them.

Bunchberry
Cornus canadensis

Color plate: Figure 29

Synonyms: Dwarf Cornel

Use: Trail nibble

Range: Open woodlands throughout New England

Similarity to toxic species: Many plants have red berries that should not be eaten. Exercise caution in identification.

Best time: Late June through September

Status: Common and abundant

Tools needed: None

The flowering dogwood tree makes spring in southern New England a visual treat. But sadly, extreme northern New England is too inhospitable for this cheery tree. There is a second best, though. That's bunchberry. The bunchberry is a low-growing perennial with flowers that mimic its showier cousin. The flowers later turn to edible bright red berries that delight children young and old.

Summer is bunchberry time. The shiny red berries are ready slightly before other more notable berries come upon the scene, and they last after the rest have withered on the vine.

Some authors refer to bunchberries as survival food, intimating that the taste is barely tolerable but anything that keeps meat on the bones is worth trying. I disagree with that attitude. Bunchberries are, to be candid, not delicious, nor are they overly sweet. But they have a mild flavor and are palatable enough to a hot, sweaty, and hungry person after a long walk through the woods. I admit that bunchberries are not good enough to pick in great quantities and take home and freeze, or to turn into jams and jellies. But for a quick pick-me-up, the ever-present bunchberry has a definite place and is well worth discovering.

Bunchberries are low growing, never more than 6 or 8 inches tall. The leaves, which are widest in the middle and have a thin, pointed tip, are arranged in a whorl of six. The leaves are deeply veined and lack teeth. The showy, four-petaled (these are not true petals, but bracts—the actual flower is just the green disc in the center) blossoms are lime green early in the season and eventually turn a bright creamy white. The berries, naturally, grow in bunches.

Wintergreen
Gaultheria procumbens

Color plate: Figure 30

Synonyms: Teaberry, Checkerberry

Use: Trail nibble

Range: Throughout New England in open woodlands

Similarity to toxic species: Many plants with red berries are toxic. Be sure of identification.

Best time: Year-round. Wintergreen berries persist over the winter, under the snow. In early spring they are literally the first wild edible of the season. The freezing process seems to make the "Wintergreen" flavor more pronounced.

Status: Common and abundant

Tools needed: None

Collecting old-time medicine and extract bottles is one of my pet passions. These are fairly common around the old farms of New England, but a bottle with its label intact is an extraordinary find. One of my favorite bottles once held extract of Wintergreen, and the somewhat yellowed label reads, "Pure Essence Checkerberry. For flavoring ice cream, custards, jellies, ices, &c. Directions: One-half teaspoonful or more to a quart according to the taste. Prepared by N. Wood and Son, 428–430 Fore Street, Portland, ME." In the nineteenth and early twentieth centuries, Portland abounded with patent medicines and natural extract bottlers. And it is apparent that back then, people appreciated the penetrating flavor of Wintergreen.

Today Wintergreen is synthesized. No longer can we go to the local general store and purchase a bottle of "Checkerberry extract." But we can still enjoy the rich taste and fragrance of Wintergreen in its natural state. It is one of our more common woodland ground covers.

Look for thick mats of Wintergreen in open woodlands. The leaves are a little more than an inch long, are shiny, and have a few fine teeth. The color of the leaf varies from green to plum red. This variation of leaf color perplexed me until one blustery morning in early spring, when I happened to push a bunch of leaf litter aside with my boot. There, before me, was my answer: The leaves that had been covered with the litter were burgundy red, but the leaves of neighboring plants, which were exposed to the light, were deep green. This has been proved to me time and time again. It would probably be possible, by way of a basic experiment, to alter the color of any particular patch of Wintergreen leaves simply by allowing or denying sunlight.

The small red berries are edible, and to the surprise of many, so are the leaves. In fact, it is the leaves that I choose to chew on during my morning woodland perambulations. The leaves should not be swallowed, but when gently chewed, they produce a perfectly wonderful Wintergreen flavor, one that the laboratory cannot quite duplicate. Oh, yes, there is something else about these delightful Wintergreen leaves: The red leaves have the best, most pronounced flavor. I thought this was my imagination at work until a friend, a veteran woodsman, brought up the point, confirming my view.

The Wintergreen flower is a tiny white bell, suspended by a thin U-shaped stem. The lip of the flower is gently scalloped. Wintergreen never gains more than an inch or so in altitude. The berries are unmistakable, though; even if you were unsure of their identification, crushing a berry will yield that familiar Wintergreen aroma.

As an aside, in the dim past my grandmother used oil of Wintergreen (along with lots of other potions and lotions, some of which I detested) on my young strains and muscle hurts. I can't remember if she diluted the stuff or not; probably she did, because it would be caustic if used straight from the bottle. And now, every time I chew a Wintergreen berry, or nibble on a fragrant leaf, my grandma's tender ministrations come to mind, warm and comfortable. That's one of the nice things about plants—they can elicit fond memories. And what is nicer than that?

Purple Trillium
Trillium undulatum

Color plate: Figure 31

Synonyms: Red Trillium, Wake-Robin, Stinking Benjamin, Birthroot

Use: Cooked vegetable, salad ingredient

Range: Shaded woodlands throughout New England

Similarity to toxic species: None

Best time: May

Status: Locally abundant, but rare in some locales. The biggest threat to Purple Trillium, along with so many other plants and animals, is not from foragers but from rampant development.

Tools needed: A jackknife or shears helps snip the leaves, but tools are not really necessary.

My decision to include Purple Trillium here was not an easy one. A member of the lily family, this is a favorite wildflower and although it is generally common, and oftentimes occurs in large colonies, the species could potentially suffer from overeager foragers, especially in areas where it is scarce to begin with. Additionally, Purple Trillium is but one of many trilliums, some of which should never be picked. That said, the careful forager might clip a leaf here and there from a colony of Purple Trilliums without doing the least bit of harm. Still, keep in mind that this is a plant that should not be harvested in any quantity; follow my lead and consider a dish of steamed Purple Trillium leaves a rite of spring, something special to look forward to each year.

    Apparently conditions are just right for Purple Trilliums in the patch of woods along my driveway. The showy leaves and burgundy red flowers put on quite a show each spring. So here is where I harvest enough leaves for a side dish or two. I prefer Purple Trillium cooked rather than raw. Both are fine, though. Harvest by snipping only one leaf from each plant until a sufficient amount has been gathered. This does not, in my experience, injure the plant. *Don't* pull up the entire plant.

For me, Purple Trillium means spring has sprung, in all its glory. When the dark red, three-petaled flowers bloom, it is time to go fishing, for the mayfly hatches have surely begun; Ostrich Fern fiddleheads are nearly past their prime, the warbler migration is ongoing, and it's time to do some serious work in the garden. And—in northern New England—the blackflies are out in force.

The leaves, petals, and sepals of Purple Trillium—indeed, all trilliums—occur in triplets. The plants stand between 6 and 16 inches tall, with the average being about 8 inches. The leaves have a puckered shape, wide in the middle and with a tapering point at the end. If one leaf is picked, the remaining two look like a circus clown's outlandish bow tie.

Purple Trilliums can also be tentatively identified by sniffing the flower, although I don't recommend this: Purple Trillium is pollinated by flies, and has the odor of rotten meat. Needless to say, it does not make a good cut flower.

Purple Trillium, particularly the root, has a long history of medical uses, especially as a cure for many women's complaints. Any malady that Purple Trillium may ameliorate, though, can be cured by other means. It isn't necessary to dig Purple Trillium root, and I discourage the folk-medicinal use of this pretty woodland plant.

Before the plant is finished flowering, clip some leaves and cook them by boiling or steaming. Cooking time is short, between eight and ten minutes. Be sure not to overcook. Drain well and serve as a side dish with a small dab of real butter.

Common Blue Violet
Viola papilionacea

Color plate: Figure 32

Synonyms: Violet

Use: Trail nibble, salad ingredient, fancy syrup

Range: Throughout New England

Similarity to toxic species: None

Best time: May and June

Status: Common

Tools needed: None

The local woodpeckers tell me when it is time to pick wild violets. During the spring mating season, male woodpeckers woo the females by drumming on anything that resonates, which can include barn doors, dead trees, aluminum boats, and metal roofs. This cacophony of sound coincides with prime violet-picking time.

Violets are not long lived when cut and placed in a small water-filled vase or jar. Even so, it is a rite of the season to grace the kitchen table with a fresh bouquet of these delicate wildflowers.

Besides being pretty, violet blossoms are eminently edible and healthful. The dainty blue blossoms are packed with vitamin C, that vitamin so necessary to human health. It's fun to pick handfuls of violet blossoms and munch them while walking. Or the blossoms, minus the stems, can be added to any salad for taste as well as appearance. Want to surprise dinner guests? Place one perfect violet blossom in each cell of an ice cube tray, fill with water, freeze, and use in drinks. This is a real conversation piece and certainly more attractive—and perhaps more nourishing—than a cocktail onion or olive.

How about violet blossom syrup? Make a sugar syrup, using the same ratio—one part sugar to two parts water—that is used to fill a hummingbird feeder. Pour the hot syrup into a glass jar filled with violet blossoms. The violets relinquish their color, and streamers of blue can be seen trailing and swirling in the hot syrup. When all color has faded from the blossoms and the syrup has cooled, strain it, add a couple of good squirts of lemon juice, and place in a dark cupboard. This syrup is a heavenly addition to crepes and pancakes. It is also soothing to scratchy throats and helps hoarseness.

Violet leaves, when young, are excellent in salads. As might be expected of any dark green leaf, they are rich in vitamin A. My favorite use is in salads, but the leaves can also be boiled for a few minutes and served as a cooked vegetable.

Violet blossoms have five petals. The petals show considerable venation. The leaves are somewhat heart shaped and are roughly toothed. Violets are from 5 to 8 inches tall.

Serviceberry
Amelanchier spp.

Color plate: Figures 33 and 34

Synonyms: Sarvisberry, Juneberry, shadberry

Use: Trail nibble, sauce, frozen fruit, addition to muffins and pancakes

Range: Throughout New England

Similarity to toxic species: None

Best time: June and July

Status: Common

Tools needed: None

The study of the serviceberry presents many conflicting views and possibilities. It is variously estimated that between twenty and twenty-five species occur in North America, but hybridizing introduces additional variations. Fortunately, all are similar in appearance and all are more or less edible. Some are better than others.

Once I heard a friend mention how pretty the Wild Cherry blossoms were that year. This was in early April, and since it would be more than a month before the different species of Wild Cherries blossomed, I knew he was referring to serviceberries. In fact, the showy white blossoms are perhaps the best means of identifying the serviceberry. In very early spring, while patches of snow hold fast in the shaded woodland ravines and gullies, serviceberry puts on a dazzling display of pure white blossoms. These make a striking contrast with the still-drab browns and grays of the season.

It is easy to spot serviceberry in bloom while driving down the highway: It is the only thing blooming. In order to gain access to different sources of serviceberries, make note of the blooming plants in spring and revisit them in late June or early July, when the berries are ripe. When I encounter blooming serviceberries on my own property, I mark the spot with blue surveyor's flagging. I don't recommend using such material on the property of others, though.

Serviceberry occurs both as a tree and a shrub. Someone once determined that anything more than 20 feet tall was a tree; less than 20 feet, a shrub. Such strict distinctions are meaningless, though, when dealing with a tree/shrub that refuses to stay within formal boundaries. Fortunately it makes little difference, so long as the fruit is sweet and tasty.

Serviceberry has another admirable characteristic: Its wood is rock hard, one of the hardest on the continent. It is sometimes used for tool handles, but since the tree is of a small diameter, it cannot be used for furniture. It has a close grain and a handsome dark brown color with traces of red.

When serviceberry approaches the 20-foot mark, the limbs become whimsically contorted, with twists and turns of every description. Sometimes the lower limbs spread out horizontally only a few feet from the ground. A big serviceberry tree reminds me of Harry Lauder's walking stick.

Serviceberry leaves look much like apple leaves—finely toothed, somewhat leathery, and fairly thin. The leaves are alternate. The tight-fitting bark is a medium gray color. The berries, which are the real prize offered by the serviceberry, look much like blueberries. Early on the berries are purplish-red; they later acquire the darkest shade of blue. Birds of every kind flock to ripe serviceberries, as do various small mammals and the young of the human species. Adults almost universally ignore the bounty of the serviceberry, although in years past country folk of all ages paid homage to this lowly plant.

There is a great deal of variation in the flavor of serviceberries. It's odd that some trees have the sweetest berries imaginable, while the fruit of others is insipid, hardly fit for the birds. The key to finding good serviceberries is to sample every tree in the area.

Once a tree bearing delicious berries is located, the berries may be put to a variety of uses. First, and as you might guess, my favorite is to eat them as is. One serviceberry tree on the windward side of Cape Jellison, Maine, has the best-tasting fruit in the world (maybe not the world, but all of Maine, anyway). To walk along the wild shore and gaze out at Penobscot Bay is pleasure enough, but add fresh, sweet serviceberries and the walk becomes a trip through a garden of earthly delights.

The berries can also be stewed. Use one part sugar to three parts berries and cook over low heat for twenty minutes, stirring occasionally. The same ratio to sugar and berries may be used to freeze the berries in freezer jars. Serviceberries can be used fresh in muffins and pancakes. They may also be dried for the same use. Make a berry dryer of a roughly 36- by 24-inch *nylon* window screen fastened to a frame of wooden lathes. Attach screw eyes at the four corners and suspend the frame from a beam in a dark attic, barn, or garage. Cover the screen with serviceberries and check them every few days, moving them around a little by hand. Discard any berries that are mushy or unripe. When completely dried, store in an airtight glass jar. Add the dried berries to pancake or muffin batter. They can also be used in old-fashioned, slow-cooking oatmeal.

~ 5 ~

Mushrooms

Eating wild mushrooms entails a degree of risk. The mushroom being collected must be positively identified as an edible variety. The consequences of a misidentification are too great to allow any room for error. A cavalier attitude has no place in the world of the wild-mushroom hunter.

The way to get a leg up on identifying and collecting wild mushrooms is to learn everything there is to know about a single common variety. Become thoroughly knowledgeable about that particular mushroom. Then learn about another type. In time it will be possible to go afield and, if conditions are right, harvest a variety of delicious wild mushrooms.

Here's another thing about wild mushrooms: Always wash them thoroughly and always eat them cooked, not raw. *Always.*

New England, especially northern New England, because of its climate and forestation, is prime habitat for wild mushrooms, with hundreds of different kinds of resident mushrooms. Of these, only a small number may be safely eaten.

No blanket statement may be made about mushroom habitat. Some, such as the various puffballs, seem to like a rather poor, gravelly soil. Others live on decaying trees and rotting stumps. And some like the acid ground so common around pine woods. It is up to the collector to know the three W's—that is, what kind of mushroom will be growing, when it will be prime, and where it will be found. After that, it's the same as anything else: Once you acquire knowledge, the subject is immediately demystified.

Besides comparing a wild mushroom to a picture in a book and comparing features from a written description, a spore print must usually be taken in order to make a positive identification. The spores can be captured and examined by placing the mushroom—gill- or pore-side down—on a piece of paper and covering it with a drinking glass. Leave the mushroom overnight. The next day, lift it up, and there will be a print of the spores.

Spore prints look much like a photographic negative (although in this case, the print is a positive). Each mushroom has a different-colored spore print. So if the book says a certain mushroom leaves a brown spore print, use white paper; brown or black paper is better for a white spore print. Spore prints are things of beauty, wondrous pictures made by nature. Even if you don't eat mushrooms, it is great fun to make and collect spore prints.

Spore print tables are not included in this book because it is not a mushroom book as such, but rather mushrooms are included here because they are fair game for foragers. Mushrooms require much detailed concentration. To become completely knowledgeable about mushrooms, buy a guide that deals specifically with them. Also find the address of your local mushroom club (these are found everywhere, in every state) and join. Go on field trips and take advantage of the club's collective experience.

I learned about mushrooms myself from friends and later made an in-depth study on my own. Now I am intimately familiar with a small number of mushrooms. These are the ones I purposely seek. Additionally, I try to add to my stable of known varieties each year. The process is painstaking, though, because it involves consulting various field guides and taking spore prints. It is impossible to be too careful when dealing with wild mushrooms.

Be careful, take nothing for granted, and study, study, study. Then a door will be opened to a remarkable new world of fascinating and oftentimes delicious wild plants. Happy hunting.

Note that the few mushrooms listed here are by no means the only edible wild mushrooms native to New England. They are but a sample, a tiny example of the great range of mushrooms to be found in our region, chosen both for their esculence and for the ease of identifying them in the field.

Morel
Morchella esculenta

Color plate: Figure 35

Synonyms: Sponge Mushroom

Use: Cooked mushroom

Range: Throughout New England

Similarity to toxic species: The False Morel, *Gyromitra esculenta,* is sometimes mistaken for a true Morel.

Best time: May

Status: Locally abundant, but scarce in some areas

Tools needed: A knife helps sever the stem close to the ground.

Morels have been my Holy Grail in the mushroom world. Although I regularly searched for them, I never saw a wild Morel near my Maine home until recently. A couple in a neighboring town, knowing my passion for wild mushrooms, called and asked me if I would like to come over and not only see but also pick a Morel. I was in their driveway almost before they had a chance to hang up the phone.

The tension was considerable; this was a lifetime search about to be consummated. I was directed to a gravelly patch of lawn and told to poke about—a lone Morel was there. And sure enough, after considerable crawling on hands and knees, there it stood, a tiny, dark gray mushroom, an honest-to-goodness Morel. I examined every aspect of this storied fungus and then reverently slid my forefinger under the stem and popped it from the ground.

Back home, the Morel lost some of its mystery. I sliced it into four pieces to make it seem like more and then sautéed it in butter. It was good—very good. As good as some of the other, more common wild mushrooms I pick regularly around home. But it wasn't quite so sacred as I had hoped.

Later, at a friend's birthday celebration, another couple told me that their lawn was filled with Morels; they had Morels to spare, to wantonly fling to people like me. It struck me as odd that Morels had been a will-o'-the-wisp to me for so long, while to these people the famed mushroom was no more or less special than an acorn.

Learn to distinguish between Morels and False Morels by noting the following characteristics. Morels have pits, and both the cap and stem are hollow. You can determine this by slicing lengthwise. False Morels have folds, or convolutions, but are not pitted. The False Morel looks sort of like a brain, whereas the true Morel resembles a sponge.

A forager lucky enough to find a bunch of Morel mushrooms might try the following recipe, courtesy of Ken Allen, and taken from his book *Cooking Wild*. This recipe might be used for any mushrooms, not only Morels.

Creamed Mushrooms on Toast

1 pound mushrooms
4–5 tablespoons butter
3 tablespoons flour
$1/2$ teaspoon salt
$1/4$ teaspoon pepper
$1/2$ cup sherry (optional)
1 cup cream

Sauté the mushrooms in the butter over low heat. When the edges brown, remove them to a warm dish. Sprinkle the flour into the pan, stirring until the butter, mushroom juices, and flour become smooth and thick. Add salt and pepper and continue cooking. This is important, because uncooked flour in a subtle dish such as this one actually imparts a flour taste. Before the flour browns from the heat, add the sherry, if you wish, and simmer until most of the liquid has evaporated. Add the cream and stir until it reaches the desired thickness. Then return the sautéed mushrooms to the pan, and reheat them. Serve on toasted, homemade white bread.

If Morels are scarce, which is more than likely, slice them lengthwise and gently and slowly cook in real butter. This may take twenty minutes or more, but don't hurry the process.

Morels are where you find them. Good luck in the quest.

Chicken of the Woods
Laetiporus sulphureus

Color plate: Figure 36

Synonyms: Sulfur Shelf

Use: A fine cooked mushroom

Range: Throughout New England

Similarity to toxic species: None

Best time: September and October

Status: Common

Tools needed: None for picking, but Chicken of the Woods oftentimes occurs in huge quantities; bring a cardboard box or large canvas sack to hold the bounty.

I've been told that Chicken of the Woods gets its name from its flavor—it's said to taste like chicken. I know a few things that taste like chicken, but this isn't one of them. Still, properly sautéed in butter, Chicken of the Woods, does taste a little like lobster. But lobsters don't live in the woods, and maybe that's why the anonymous mycophile who named this mushroom chose chicken instead. The flesh is meaty, though, much like lobster flesh.

Chicken of the Woods is a shelf mushroom and grows on injured or dying hardwood trees. It isn't uncommon, but in my area it has the maddening habit of growing best in the yards of people who never pick the stuff, but won't allow others the privilege. Chicken of the Woods also grows on wooded property, generally where every other tree is posted with intimidating NO-TRESPASSING signs. These signs rarely carry the name of the landowner, so it's impossible to call or visit and seek permission to pick the mushroom. Once in a great while, a colony of Chicken of the Woods is spotted on land where public access is allowed. These are places to remember.

One fall, during a futile wild-cranberry expedition, I pulled my canoe ashore, sat on a log, and marveled at the striking brilliance of the fall foliage around the surrounding wetland and nearby hardwood ridges. It was enough to be alive and well on such a day, to be immersed in this kaleidoscope of color. Then, as if in reward for a humble attitude, I looked behind me and there, on a dead Black Cherry tree, was a huge Chicken of the Woods mushroom. Suddenly cranberries didn't matter a whit. Nature had provided.

Chicken of the Woods, it should be pointed out, is so easily identified that it is a perfect "beginner" mushroom. It's a bracket-type mushroom and grows in giant clusters. The bottom of the cap has pores rather than gills, and the top is smooth and somewhat fluted. The margins are slightly wavy. The color is usually bright orange, running toward a creamy yellow on the edges. The style and color of Chicken of the Woods make it recognizable even to those who would not otherwise eat a wild mushroom. This makes it a highly desired product for sale at health food stores, where the cut-up mushroom is peddled at ridiculously high prices.

Chicken of the Woods often appears on the same site, year after year. However—and this is worth noting—it doesn't always appear at the same time. My records indicate as much as a three-week spread from one year to the next. Temperature, humidity, and rainfall have much to do with the emergence of this colorful fungus. This means that once you locate a site, you should visit it regularly during the fruiting season. It doesn't take long for the mushroom to appear, reach its prime, and then dry to inedibility. Such diligent monitoring is worthwhile, however; this is one of the very finest mushrooms available.

Chicken of the Woods can be slowly simmered in real butter and served as is. Like Hen of the Woods, Chicken of the Woods must be chopped into manageable bits and thoroughly rinsed to remove any bark, wood fibers, or insects. If the mushroom is slightly older than might be hoped, the outer edge will be the most tender. Save this portion separately from the rest. This is the stuff to use for frying and in fritters. If it's not too tough, the rest can be chopped fine, and used in stews. The long, slow cooking helps tenderize the mushroom. I retain all but the toughest portions of Chicken of the Woods because the flavor is so satisfying even if the mushroom is a bit chewy.

Once picked, Chicken of the Woods stores well in the refrigerator crisper.

Hen of the Woods
Grifolia frondosa

Color plate: Figure 37

Use: An excellent mushroom when cooked

Range: Throughout New England

Similarity to toxic species: None, but with all mushrooms be certain about your identification.

Best time: September and October

Status: Common

Tools needed: A knife will help cut base of the mushroom from the host stump, but the mushroom can also be picked by hand.

A lone oak stump on a gravel road in the rolling hills of Mid-Coast Maine once hosted spores of the Hen of the Woods mushroom. Each fall some friends who live just down the road from this treasure trove would call me when the mushrooms were at their prime, and we would pick pounds of the rubbery polypore.

But our annual Hen of the Woods harvest was soon to be a thing of the past. The local snowplow man was annoyed because his plow blade often came up short on the mushroom stump. So the following spring a backhoe dug out all traces of it. And that fall, when we should have reveled in many pounds of Hen of the Woods, there were none to be found.

Since then, another stump along another road has provided us with our Hen of the Woods. Eventually that stump, too, will be history and we will have to find an alternate source. But that's mushrooming.

The Hen of the Woods looks rather like a big, brown coral. The chestnut brown, cream-streaked caps are attached to a thick, fleshy base. The tops of the caps are relatively smooth, with minute pores located on the undersides. The mushroom has a rubbery texture.

The Hen of the Woods and a similar mushroom called Many-Capped Polypore, *G. umbellata,* are nearly identical in appearance, and both are perfectly edible. Both are common in New England.

This mushroom needs some preparation before being eaten or preserved. Hen of the Woods must be cut up into fairly small pieces—say, half the size of the average potato chip—because it is somewhat tough. That accomplished, the list of what can be done with this versatile mushroom is practically endless.

First, it is excellent fried. This is one mushroom that wants to be fried for more than just a few minutes. It need not be cooked to a crisp, but at least fifteen minutes of slow cooking is needed. I like to add half an ounce of sherry and perhaps a dash of Angostura bitters to the pan when cooking Hen of the Woods. That's my taste, though, and such extras aren't necessary. Next, the Hen of the Woods is a superior soup and stew ingredient, imparting both an interesting texture and a slightly bitter taste—this is the dandelion of the mushroom world—that contrasts wonderfully with the other ingredients. Any casserole can benefit by the addition of half a cup of chopped Hen of the Woods.

How about scrambled eggs and Hen of the Woods mushrooms? It's a breakfast treat that people would fight over (in fact, I am told by an Italian friend that in Italy, where Hen of the Woods also grows, violence has erupted over proprietary rights to prime mushroom sites). Cook the mushrooms first; when they are tender, pour in two beaten eggs. Stir and serve with any good Louisiana hot sauce. Mercy, it's good. Omelets can also be elevated to the heavenly realms when Hen of the Woods is added to the mix.

Hen of the Woods freezes well. The accepted way to freeze mushrooms is to sauté them in butter or margarine, allow them to cool, and then put them in plastic freezer bags. This is fine, but what about folks who must not eat fatty, fried foods? The answer came to me recently when I had a big supply of Hen of the Woods and, being gun-shy about putting an entire year's supply of mushrooms in the freezer (the electrical power grid where I live is not dependable, and a few years ago I lost nearly my whole freezer of food during an ice storm), I decided to experiment and see if the mushrooms would benefit by home canning.

The mushrooms were packed in good old well water and processed according to directions. The finished product was actually more flavorful than the fried mushrooms. And the slight bitter taste inherent in Hen of the Woods? Gone.

Sometime next September, begin the search for a stump that harbors Hen of the Woods mushrooms. With luck, the site should produce for many years. That is, unless the local snowplow man develops a grudge against it.

Goose Tongue
Plantago juncoides

Figure 1

Orache
Atriplex patula

Figure 2

Sea Blite
Suaeda maritima

Figure 3

Beach Peas
Lathyrus japonicus

Figure 4

Sea-Rocket
Cakile edentula

Figure 5

Glasswort
Salicornia spp.

Figure 6

Silverweed
Potentilla anserina

Figure 7

Northern Bay
Myrica pensylvanica

Figure 8

Wrinkled Rose
Rosa rugosa

Figure 9

Ostrich Fern
Pteretis pensylvanica

Figure 10

Ostrich Fern

Figure 11

Stinging Nettles
Urtica dioica

Figure 12

Curled Dock
Rumex crispus

Figure 13

Curled Dock

Figure 14

Seedstalk, fall/winter

Wild Oats
Uvularia sessilifolia

Figure 15

Marsh Marigold
Caltha palustris

Figure 16

Lamb's-Quarters
Chenopodium album

Figure 17

Lamb's-Quarters

Figure 18

Quickweed
Galinsoga ciliata

Figure 19

Field Peppergrass
Lepidium campestre

Figure 20

Green Amaranth
Amaranthus retroflexus

Figure 21

Purslane
Portulaca oleracea

Figure 22

Lady's Thumb
Polygonum persicaria

Figure 23

Clintonia
Clintonia borealis

Figure 24

Indian Cucumber
Medeola virginica

Figure 25

View of white root and berries

Indian Cucumber

Figure 26

View of whorled leaf

Large-Leafed Aster
Aster macrophyllus

Figure 27

Seedstalk, late summer/early fall

Large-Leafed Aster

Figure 28

Mature plant in summer

Bunchberry
Cornus canadensis

Figure 29

Wintergreen
Gaultheria procumbens

Figure 30

Purple Trillium
Trillium undulatum

Figure 31

Common Blue Violet
Viola papilionacea

Figure 32

Serviceberry
Amelanchier spp.

Figure 33

The twisted trunks of the serviceberry

Serviceberry

Figure 34

The berries resemble long-stemmed blueberries.

Morel
Morchella esculenta

Figure 35

Chicken of the Woods
Laetiporus sulphureus

Figure 36

Hen of the Woods
Grifolia frondosa

Figure 37

Common Blue Violet
Viola papilionacea

Figure 32

Serviceberry
Amelanchier spp.

Figure 33

The twisted trunks of the serviceberry

Serviceberry

Figure 34

The berries resemble long-stemmed blueberries.

Morel
Morchella esculenta

Figure 35

Chicken of the Woods
Laetiporus sulphureus

Figure 36

Hen of the Woods
Grifolia frondosa

Figure 37

Puffball
Calvatia gigantea

Figure 38

Puffball

Figure 39

Oyster Mushroom
Pleurotus ostreatus

Figure 40

Cattail
Typha latifolia

Figure 41

Cattail

Figure 42

The edible white stalks

Pickerelweed
Pontederia cordata

Figure 43

Wild Cranberry
Vaccinium macrocarpon

Figure 44

White Pine
Pinus strobus

Figure 45

Eastern Hemlock
Tsuga canadensis

Figure 46

Needles and cones

Eastern Hemlock

Figure 47

Red Spruce
Picea rubens

Figure 48

Black Willow
Salix niger

Figure 49

Valerian
Valeriana officinalis

Figure 50

Sarsaparilla
Aralia nudicaulis

Figure 51

Plant in spring

Sarsaparilla

Figure 52

Plant in summer

Yarrow
Achillea millefolium

Figure 53

Boneset
Eupatorium perfoliatum

Figure 54

Heal-All
Prunella vulgaris

Figure 55

Common Saint-John's-Wort
Hypericum perforatum

Figure 56

Canada Goldenrod
Solidago canadensis

Figure 57

Goldthread
Coptis groenlandica

Figure 58

Spotted Joe-Pye Weed
Eupatorium maculatum

Figure 59

Mugwort
Artemisia vulgaris

Figure 60

Mugwort

Figure 61

Japanese Knotweed
Polygonum cuspidatum

Figure 62

Japanese Knotweed

Figure 63

Dead stalks of the previous year's plant makes the Japanese Knotweed easy to spot.

Jewelweed
Impatiens capensis

Figure 64

Common Milkweed
Asclepias syriaca

Figure 65

Seedpods

Common Milkweed

Figure 66

Showing the tender tips

Great Burdock
Arctium lappa

Figure 67

Orpine
Sedum purpureum

Figure 68

Evening Primrose
Oenothera biennis

Figure 69

Basal rosette, early spring

Evening Primrose

Figure 70

View of root, early spring

Evening Primrose

Figure 71

Flower stalk, late summer/early fall

Pineapple Weed
Matricaria matricarioides

Figure 72

Pineapple Weed

Figure 73

Common Plantain
Plantago major

Figure 74

Blackberries
Rubus spp.

Figure 75

Highbush Cranberry
Viburnum trilobum

Figure 76

Sweetfern
Comptonia peregrina

Figure 77

Dandelion
Taraxacum officinale

Figure 78

Ground Ivy
Glechoma hederacea

Figure 79

New England
Aster
Aster novae-angliae

Figure 80

Crayfish
Decapoda astacus

Figure 81

Bullfrog
Rana catesbeiana

Figure 82

Freshwater Mussels

Figure 83

Common Blue Mussel
Mytilus edulis

Figure 84

Periwinkle
Littorina littorea

Figure 85

Atlantic Razor Clam

Ensis directus

Figure 86

Surf Clam

Spisula solidissima

Figure 87

Puffball
Calvatia gigantea (and other *Calvatia* species);
Gem-Studded Puffball, *Lycoperdon perlatum*

Color plate: Figures 38 and 39

Use: Cooked mushroom. Do not eat wild mushrooms raw.

Range: Common throughout New England

Similarity to toxic species: The developing *Amanita phalloides*, a highly toxic mushroom variety, might be confused with a puffball by a careless collector.

Best time: September and October

Status: Common and abundant

Tools needed: None

Every child intuitively knows how puffball mushrooms got their name. Step on a ripe one and out puffs a cloud of "smoke." Puffball flesh eventually changes to dark brown spores; it is these spores that produce the dense cloud every time the puffball is stepped on or agitated.

It is important to remember that only immature puffballs—those whose flesh has not yet turned to spores—with pure white flesh are edible. The majority of puffballs fall within this wide category, but there is an exception. The Hard-Skinned Puffball, *Scleroderma citrinum*, has purplish black flesh except when very young; then it has white flesh. This hard-skinned variety is easy to spot, even without examining the flesh; no other puffball has a textured, warty surface. Besides the rough, hard surface and the black interior, the Hard-Skinned Puffball is denser and weighs more than other puffballs of the same size. It is easy to recognize and therefore easy to avoid.

The acid test of any puffball is to slice it lengthwise and look at the exposed flesh. If the vague form of a cap-style mushroom is evident, it may be a young Amanita. Cap-style mushrooms have a stem, however, and since there is no true stem on a puffball (it has roots instead, and is puckered on the bottom), the difference should be readily apparent. In the end, if the puffball half exhibits pure white flesh that is the consistency of cheese, it is a good one.

Now that all the warnings have been given, once you learn to identify a puffball, it is easy to spot them even from far away. Indeed, they are perfect beginner mushrooms because they are so easy to identify. The giant puffball and some of the smaller, softball-sized puffballs of the same genus stand out like a sore thumb once your eye is trained and you know what to look for. One of my preferred modes of hunting giant puffballs is to slowly drive down what I call "puffball alley"—a stretch of country road that hosts great numbers of puffballs each year. It's lazy man's mushrooming, this, because all I have to do is stop, get out of the car, pick the mushroom, and drive on. Besides along the roadsides, look for puffballs, both the giant kind and the gem-studded type, on the poorest land around, on old lawns that have never been fertilized, on gravelly lots, and even around the edge of gravel pits.

Puffballs literally come up overnight. When I was a boy, a giant puffball the size of a jumbo loaf of white bread once magically appeared on our back lawn. The old farmer down the road wanted it, and Grandpa let him have it. Grandpa was afraid of mushrooms and didn't dare experiment with them—a wise move on his part, in view of his lack of knowledge of the different fungi.

Of the two groups of puffballs featured in this chapter, the gem-studded variety is my favorite. Gem-Studded Puffballs are particularly easy to spot because of two features. First, they are covered with lots of small, rubbery spines (the "gems"). These are easily rubbed off with the finger. The second feature is the unique pear shape. With only a modest stretching of the imagination, you might say these fungi are minaret shaped. Gem-Studded Puffballs rarely exceed 1 inch in width (this being at the top, the widest part) and perhaps 2 inches in height.

Oftentimes, these mushrooms grow in solid drifts. It is possible, then, to pick several quarts in a matter of a few minutes. Whenever I run across such a jackpot, the question of what's for dinner is rendered moot. Whatever else is on the menu, Gem-Studded Puffballs will take center stage.

The easiest way to prepare these little mushrooms is to slice them in half and fry them in butter or margarine. For me, this is standard treatment for all mushrooms. It is also the prescribed way to prepare surplus mushrooms for freezing. But what about folks who don't want to use margarine and butter? I can recommend simmering the fresh or frozen puffballs in chipotle sauce. This is a low-heat chili sauce made of vinegar, molasses, onions, chipotle chiles, and olive oil. It is mostly used as a barbecue or steak sauce, but works well for frying mushrooms because it doesn't scorch and stick to the pan. It would be possible to substitute any similar steak or barbecue sauce that exhibits similar properties. But since Gem-Studded Puffballs are somewhat mild, the chiles and other flavors in a chipotle sauce transport them from simply good to the realm of magnificent.

To prepare mushrooms for freezing, I have found that simmering them in plain water works well. They can later be fried in the medium of choice. It is not necessary to thaw mushrooms before cooking, as long as they are allowed to simmer over low heat. Talk about fast food!

The giant puffballs, which I mentioned earlier, along with other members of their clan—one of which is skull shaped, another cup shaped—are all treated similarly. The outer skin, which can become tough with age, is removed and the mushroom is sliced like a loaf of bread. These are never better than when fresh. They can be kept in the freezer, but the taste becomes too strong for my liking.

Start with a large platter of freshly sliced giant puffballs. Put some white flour in a small paper bag and add a handful of the sliced mushrooms. Blow up the bag and shake, in order to evenly coat the mushroom slices. Now slowly cook the coated slices in real butter until they are a golden brown. Serve immediately.

Both Gem-Studded Puffballs and giant puffballs are early-season mushrooms. Begin searching for them in late August, especially after a wet spell.

Finally, nearly every old-time New England farmer knew to collect the mature puffballs—the kind that puff when squeezed—in fall. These were stored in strategic spots around the barn. When an animal cut itself, it was easy to grab a puffball, aim it at the wound, and squeeze. The spores have styptic properties and stop all but the worst bleeding. They are also sterile and help ward off infection.

Oyster Mushroom
Pleurotus ostreatus

Color plate: Figure 40

Use: Cooked mushroom

Range: Throughout New England

Similarity to toxic species: None

Best time: October and November

Status: Locally abundant

Tools needed: None

The Oyster Mushroom is so called because it is shaped like an oyster shell, not because it tastes like oysters (which it doesn't). This is one of my favorite mushrooms because of its sweet, satisfying flavor. Unfortunately, mushrooms are not the most dependable crop; some years Oyster Mushrooms fail to emerge in any appreciable numbers.

Oyster Mushrooms grow on dead trees and old, rotting stumps. They begin as tiny, wee little white specks in early October, and by mid-November are an inch or so wide. This is a scale-type mushroom; the gills are on the bottom, facing the ground. A colony of Oyster Mushrooms is often tightly packed, with individuals alongside, above, and below each other in layers. The top of the creamy white "oyster" is waxy feeling.

A deep glen at the far end of my woodlot is home to a couple of colonies of Oyster Mushrooms. One of these is on its way out—the stump the Oysters live on is almost completely rotted and returned to the ground. The other colony is on a relatively intact stump. These mushrooms need to be carefully monitored so as to be harvested at the peak of perfection. This gives me a good excuse to take shotgun in hand and, with the best of intentions, walk "out back" for a few grouse and a mess of mushrooms. In truth, though, I've only hit the grouse-mushroom jackpot once. My aging bird dog, Ben, flushed a beautiful, male ruffed grouse and I made a picture-perfect shot. Ben fetched the grouse, which I stuffed in the game pouch of my canvas hunting coat. Then, without moving more than a few feet, I knelt down and harvested several pounds of perfect Oyster Mushrooms. It just doesn't get any better than that.

But now Ben is gone and the Oyster Mushroom colony has lost its vigor. It's time for me to move on, time to find another stump or dead tree that hosts a colony of sweet, mild Oyster Mushrooms.

Carefully wash the mushrooms, because bits of the dead stump might be attached at the stem, and perhaps specks of debris are trapped in the gills. Then, without further preparation, gently sauté the Oysters in real butter, being careful not to let them brown overly much. If I had to make a choice between Oyster Mushrooms and Morels, I would always choose the Oysters, hands down. That's how good they are!

— 6 —

Plants of Swamps, Bogs, and Slow-Moving Streams

Some plants must grow where it is wet, some on the moist ground, and some in the water. Marsh Marigolds, cattails, Pickerelweed, and Wild Cranberries are only a representative sample of such moisture-loving plants.

In New England, every bog or sluggish stream hosts at least some useful plants. Sometimes, such areas are not easily visited. Hip boots, or even a boat or canoe, are needed to get to where the plants grow. But these places are a different world from what we are used to. Besides the plants, various fish, insects, birds, and amphibians make swamps, bogs, and sluggish streams home. Even in the midst of industrial and urban areas, the wet spots offer a home to a plethora of interesting plants and animals. The forager knows this and cherishes such places for the beauty and diversity they represent.

Cattail
Typha latifolia

Color plate: Figures 41 and 42

Synonyms: Cat-o'-Nine-Tails

Use: Cooked vegetable, flour additive, salad ingredient, trail nibble

Range: Widespread throughout New England

Similarity to toxic species: None

Best time: Cattails are best and easiest to harvest in spring, summer, and fall, but they're also available in winter as emergency food.

Status: Common

Tools needed: To dig roots in early spring, a hand trowel or garden spade is a help, as is a jackknife to cut the sprouts and later the young shoots and flower spikes.

Kids and cattails go together. Whether it's using the dried flower heads as ersatz torches, or shaking the stalk so the wind catches the downy seeds and sets them slowly adrift, the Common Cattail has a magnetic appeal to young ones. Perhaps the cattail's preferred location—wet areas, with the accompanying life-forms such as frogs, dragonflies, and noisy red-winged blackbirds—adds to the plant's universal attraction. With that in mind, what better wild food plant might anyone choose to introduce a child to the art of foraging?

Eating cattails is not a New England tradition, at least among the European community. For the Native Americans, however, it's a different story. I once watched, spellbound, as a member of Maine's Penobscot Indian tribe taught a group of youngsters how to find, prepare, and eat cattail stalks. This was at a living-history demonstration; the kids also got to ride in a real birch-bark canoe and visit a shelter sheathed with birch bark. The cattails, though, seemed to make the biggest impression. And whether or not those children ever make a traditional shelter or attempt to fashion a birch-bark canoe later in life, they will always know how to eat a cattail.

Cattails, both the common and the narrow-leaved variety, *T. angustifolia*, have a multitude of uses throughout the growing season. In early spring, when ice still clings to the edges of small ponds and the first wood frog bravely utters its initial, staccato croak of the season, the first cattail product is ready for harvest. These are the dormant sprouts, which, if not picked, will produce another crop of cattails. The sprouts range up to 1 inch long, are white and smooth, and are shaped like the spur on a rooster's foot.

To harvest the cattail sprouts requires some determination. Knee-length rubber boots are a must, for it is usually necessary to wade out in the still-icy water and pull the old, dead cattail clumps from the protesting muck. The sprouts are attached at the ends of the roots and may be removed by hand, but are best severed with a jackknife. They may be rinsed in clean water and eaten raw, tossed in a salad (my favorite use, naturally), or steamed or boiled until tender and used as a cooked vegetable. Cattail sprouts make an interesting addition to the usual bean sprouts in an Oriental stir-fry. Harvesting a mess of cattail sprouts is an invigorating way to welcome spring.

The next cattail product is available in late spring, when the plants are from 1 to 3 feet high. These are the young shoots (immature stalks). While they can be pulled from the mud by hand, it is much easier to cut them at the base of the plant. Next, the shoots need to be trimmed in order to expose the pure white stalk inside. It is interesting to note that the shoots, or stalks, are similar in style to a leek; that is, they grow in layers, with the outer layer being tough and the inner layers tender and delicate.

At any rate, the young shoots are a wonderful, versatile vegetable. They can be eaten raw, immediately after picking, so they qualify as a trail nibble. Or they might be sliced into short lengths in which they can star as the main ingredient in a unique stir-fry. Finally, they are a fine cooked vegetable when boiled or steamed for ten minutes, drained, and served with butter, salt, and pepper.

After the cattail plant reaches maturity, it offers yet another food product. This is the "cattail" itself, which is really the pistillate, or female flower spike. The staminate, or male flower spike, is found directly above the female, giving a two-layered appearance. It is the more substantial, female flower spike that serves the forager now.

The cigar-shaped flower spike can be eaten over quite a long period but is best harvested when the surface can be easily crumbled with the thumbnail. If the flower spike is picked while still encased in its parchment-like

Plants of Swamps, Bogs, and Slow-Moving Streams

sheath, it will be a bit tough and somewhat insipid. Use the thumbnail test to determine readiness.

Using a jackknife, cut as many flower spikes as needed. As an aside, one of my favorite cattail marshes recently fell victim to a shopping center. But, no doubt by accident, the developers allowed part of the marsh to remain. Now I park in a paved parking lot and pick my cattail spikes within a stone's throw from my car. I wonder what shoppers think the weird guy with hip boots and canvas bag is doing in that "nasty" swamp?

Anyway, the flower spikes are easy to prepare. Just steam or boil for ten minutes and season with butter, salt, and pepper. Eat them just like corn on the cob. The only inedible part is the "cob," or thin, inner spike. The spikes have a sweet, nutty flavor. I always freeze a few packages for winter use. They keep well for a year or more.

Finally, the flower spikes eventually become coated with a thick layer of yellow pollen. It is absurdly simple to gather great quantities of this pollen. Bend the flower spike over a large paper bag and give it a sharp tap. Clouds of pollen will fall in the bag. At home, spread this pollen out on a clean newspaper to allow any insects the opportunity to depart. Then store it in a closed container. This pollen can be added, on a half-and-half basis, to wheat flour. It imparts an interesting flavor and pretty color to pancakes, biscuits, and muffins. Or it could be used to coat fish fillets before frying. But don't just follow my directions—be innovative. That's half the fun of dealing with wild foods.

By the way, there is no need to worry about harming a stand of cattails by harvesting them. Harvesting is equivalent to cultivation and stimulates, rather than hinders, growth.

Pickerelweed
Pontederia cordata

Color plate: Figure 43

Use: Trail nibble, cereal ingredient, cooked vegetable

Range: Throughout New England

Similarity to toxic species: None

Best time: May through September

Status: Common and abundant

Tools needed: None

Pickerelweed reminds me of bass fishing with my grandpa. Although Grandpa told me early on that this abundant weed was edible, we never bothered to pick any because every time we encountered Pickerelweed, we were engrossed in another pursuit: bass fishing. In our part of Maine, when the young Pickerelweed leaves protrude above the water's surface, the bass fishing is at its finest.

So it wasn't until the old man was long gone that I decided to try Pickerelweed. It was in September and I was, of all things, pickerel fishing. I recalled that the flower spikes were covered with little nutlike seeds. I tried a handful and wasn't awfully impressed. They tasted good enough, but did not inspire me. All the same, I picked enough to take home and dry. The dried product is a different story. These are nutty and pleasantly crunchy. They are good as out-of-hand nibbles, or they can be added to any dry cereal or to a granola mixture. I'm sure an innovative forager could come up with lots of other uses for these rough-looking seeds.

The leaves are used as a potherb and are best gathered when young, before they unfurl. Boil for ten minutes and serve with butter, salt, and pepper. I must admit that since it requires a boat or canoe to harvest these wildlings, and since every time I am in a boat or canoe the urge to fish overpowers all other intentions, my acquaintance with cooked Pickerelweed leaves is limited. Perhaps someday my priorities can be adjusted and I will remember to stop and pick a mess of Pickerelweed leaves by force of habit. I'm working on it, anyway.

Pickerelweed, when mature, has smooth, dark green, arrowhead-shaped leaves. The flower spikes, in summer, are covered with pretty little violet-blue flowers. These must be rubbed off before eating the nutty seeds. Pickerelweed grows in profuse colonies along the edges of slow-moving streams and in shallow, weedy ponds.

Wild Cranberry
Vaccinium macrocarpon

Color plate: Figure 44

Use: Sauce, jelly, juice, relish, stuffing, and muffin ingredient

Range: Throughout New England

Similarity to toxic species: None

Best time: September

Status: Common

Tools needed: None

Wild Cranberries are about the same size and shape of, and taste the same as, the commercially raised variety. The difference is that the Wild Cranberries are free and, as a wild product, are better for the spirit; for me, it means more to go to a cranberry bog and gather a year's supply of cranberries than it does to go to the store and buy them. Besides, early fall in a New England cranberry bog is a time of brilliant, contrasting colors, something well worth taking along a camera for to capture on film. Hardly anyone ever feels the desire to take color photos of the produce aisle of the local supermarket.

A sluggish, winding stream bisects my favorite cranberry bog. An old White brand, 17-foot fiberglass canoe is my ticket to this magical place. Since an independent electric power producer now controls this stream, the chances of hitting the cranberries are hit or miss. Oftentimes the dam owner floods the stream in fall, leaving the cranberries under a foot of water. Other times he turns the stream to a tiny trickle, and the moisture-loving berries wither and die. But some years, he manages not to harm the berries. This is my time to gather gallons of the tart red fruits.

This bog was once commercially harvested, so an old-timer told me. Children would be paid so much a gallon to harvest the berries with blueberry rakes—wide boxes with a serrated mouth that pick berries, leaves, and sticks all at the same time. Now only die-hard foragers like me venture out on the bog in search of cranberries.

In Maine, mid-September is the time to pick the berries. Most are almost but not quite ripe at this time. That's fine, because the unripe berries will slowly ripen in a cardboard box at home, much like a partially green tomato. It is easy to pick a few gallons of berries with the fingers. And who would want more than a few gallons of cranberries anyway?

The Wild Cranberry is a vining plant, with short, alternate, paddle-shaped leaves. The berries are about $1/2$ inch or less in diameter. When ripe, they may retain a trace of yellow, but this does not hurt their flavor. Fully ripe or overripe fruits are a dark red.

Cranberries may be stored in a cool place for many weeks. If many of the berries are only about half red, it is a good idea to check them every other day, removing the ripe berries and separating them from the rest. Cranberries keep frozen, in the freezer, literally for years. To freeze cranberries, first rinse them, allow the berries to dry, and put them in freezer bags. No blanching is required. Cranberries can also be dried.

My favorite use of Wild Cranberries, fresh or frozen, is in a sauce. Put whole cranberries in a saucepan and add water until they float. Bring to a boil, stir, and add sugar, a tablespoon at a time, tasting frequently. It is important not to add so much sugar that the tart "cranberry" taste is destroyed. Once adequate sugar has been stirred in, allow the pot to simmer, stirring occasionally. As they cook, the berries will pop with a snapping sound. After ten minutes of simmering, allow the berries to cool and then put them in the refrigerator. The liquid will jell, making a true sauce. This is a whole-cranberry sauce. A smoother sauce more like the canned variety can be made by putting the berries through a food mill.

Fresh, frozen, or dried cranberries can be added to a muffin mix. When eaten as part of a muffin, cranberries don't seem so tart. Cranberry muffins are, in fact, my favorite kind.

Sometimes fortune favors my bird-hunting efforts with a fresh grouse or two. I like to treat these birds royally, and that means gently plucking the feathers, rather than skinning them, as most New England hunters do. And for the crowning touch, I stuff the grouse with a dressing made from homemade bread crumbs, chunks of peeled apple, a home-grown spice mixture of thyme, basil, and oregano, some chopped Wild Cranberries, and enough water to make the mass stick together. The amount of each ingredient varies according to taste. The bird (or birds) is roasted in a medium oven until the breast can be cut with a fork and no red shows.

Cranberries can also be used in standard jelly and relish recipes. The resulting product is colorful and tangy.

Finally, although September is cranberry month in New England, it is possible to find overwintered cranberries in early spring. These are soft but still edible. I even eat a few of these carryover cranberries raw when I find them. They're a greeting from a past season, a sign of the continuing flow of nature's bounty.

7

Trees

Trees are the ultimate plant. The largest plants on the planet, they furnish us with fruit, nuts, and lumber to build our homes. And yet foragers often fail to regard trees as proper objects of their avocation. Talk about not seeing the forest for the trees!

Trees offer many products that can be harvested year-round. That sets them head and shoulders (or perhaps crown and branch) above most of the other useful plants. Here are a few for-instances.

The list of medicines from trees is practically endless. Then again, certain parts of trees have multitudes of utilitarian uses. Consider that Red Spruce roots were once used to sew birch bark together when making containers, baskets, and even canoes. Some trees can be worked up into splints, which are used as weavers for baskets and even chair backs and bottoms. Cedar oil was once harvested commercially. The winged seeds from maple trees contain edible, nutlike product; the inner bark of many trees can be used, in a pinch, as an emergency food. It is certain that foragers need to examine trees more closely.

White Pine
Pinus strobus

Color plate: Figure 45

Use: Healthful tea

Range: Throughout New England

Similarity to toxic species: None

Best time: Year-round

Status: Common

Tools needed: None

Trees are not the first item that comes to mind when considering wild foods. And yet the stately White Pine is the source of a healthful and, to my taste, pleasant, tea. The White Pine is the official tree of the state of Maine. That state, once the province of Maine, has a long maritime history. White Pine figures into this history because it was this species that provided the straight, tall masts for the old sailing ships. In fact, in 1691, because of a scarcity of ship's masts in the old country, the British Crown declared that all White Pine trees of at least 24 inches in diameter, standing within three miles of the sea, were the "King's Pines" and, as such, were off-limits to colonists. The king may as well have told those independent New England folk that they could no longer shoot bears, catch codfish, or drink rum; the King's Pines continued to run through New England sawmills despite the silly English dictate.

The King's Pines were identified as such by being blazed with the sign of the "broad arrow." Interestingly, as late as the middle of the last century, these marks are reputed to be legible on certain ancient pine trees in Maine. In fact, one of my buddies tells me that when he way a boy in the early 1950s, a local woodsman in his native Machias, Maine, showed him a giant of an old pine with the plainly visible mark of the broad arrow. I believe him.

White Pines reputedly have numerous uses, most of which involve considerable work for a rather poor return. The single, most important use, though—other than lumber—is to make a healthful tea of the tree's green needles. These are easy to gather: Simply pull them from the branches. To make the tea, finely chop enough needles to fill a teacup about one-third full. Add boiling water, let steep, and enjoy. Honey or even sugar can be added, but I would ask that the tea be tried "neat" first, before adding any sweetener.

White Pine is a rich source of vitamin C and a good source of vitamin A. With such readily available sources of these useful vitamins growing all around us, it seems like a poor plan to pay money for synthetic vitamins.

Young White Pines have a fairly smooth gray-green bark. Older trees have thick, grayish bark, with considerable fissuring. The needles, really the tree's leaves, grow in clusters of five, making for easy identification. To help remember this, just remember that the first half of White Pine's name has five letters, as do the leaves. You can't go wrong.

Eastern Hemlock
Tsuga canadensis

Color plate: Figures 46 and 47

Use: Tea

Range: Throughout New England

Similarity to toxic species: American Yew, *Taxus canadensis,* is a small (3 feet tall) shrub with red berries. The berries contain a single, poisonous seed. The foliage is toxic in certain stages. The needles of the yew resemble those of Eastern Hemlock, but the similarity ends there; foragers should have no difficulty in discerning the difference between the mighty Eastern Hemlock tree and the American Yew, a commonly cultivated shrub.

Best time: Year-round

Status: Common

Tools needed: None

In earlier days, the typical image of a New England woodsman was of a hearty individual who wore wool pants, a knit hat, and a red-and-black-checkered shirt. This rugged soul carried a double-bitted axe and had a small teakettle fastened to his belt. The teakettle was used for the obligatory cup of hemlock tea at noontime.

Did the old-timers know that hemlock-needle tea was rich in vitamin C, and that it could help any number of ailments if taken in quantity? Possibly they intuited that this easily obtained beverage was good for them. But more likely, they drank it because they liked it. And that's mostly why I drink it. I also like the idea of a link between me and those old woodsmen. . . . It's like living in the old days, each time I have a hot cup of hemlock tea.

Scholars should note that the Eastern Hemlock is in no way related to the hemlock that killed Socrates. His ill brew was made from a small, perennial plant belonging to the carrot family.

Mature trees will stand between 50 and 70 feet tall. The needles measure about $1/3$ inch and are flat. They are not at all stiff or prickly, and are shorter toward the tip of the twig. The needles are attached by means of a short petiole. The cones measure about ¾ inch and are attached by tiny, thin stems. The bark is rough, with lots of ridges, and ranges in color from dark gray to red ochre.

Everyone who spends much time in the North Woods knows that the snow is never as deep under a hemlock tree as in other parts of the woods. Perhaps the way the flat needles are arranged helps deflect the snow. Wildlife, especially deer, are aware of the sanctuary afforded by hemlock trees and are quick to take advantage of it.

To make hemlock tea, simply pull a handful of fresh needles from a green twig, place them in a cup, and cover with boiling water. Wouldn't it be nice to go in the woods on some cold winter day, build a campfire, and, as the old-timers used to say, "byle up a kittle" of hemlock tea? Sometimes it is possible to bring back the old days!

Red Spruce
Picea rubens

Color plate: Figure 48

Use: Chewing gum

Range: Throughout the region

Similarity to toxic species: None

Best time: Anytime the sap is not frozen

Status: Common

Tools needed: Any knife with a heavy blade. A Boy Scout–type jackknife is ideal.

One of my favorite hikes leads to a barren, rocky mountaintop overlooking Maine's Penobscot Bay. The trail runs gradually uphill for about a mile to a plateau. From there, it becomes steep for the short climb to the summit. It's at this point that the aroma of Red Spruce envelops the hiker. It is virtually impossible to continue on without pausing to inhale the fragrant, almost overpowering spruce perfume. Many of the trees here have scars where limbs have been broken during times of high wind. From these scars flows the resinous sap that eventually hardens into the product woods-wise folks know as spruce gum.

At one point a Maine company made and distributed spruce gum. The gum was rendered, and impurities such as moss and sticks were removed. Then it was fashioned into little round balls and coated with cornstarch before being packaged. It saddened me greatly when the last box of spruce gum left the shelves of our local stores. It helped to know that I could still go in the woods and get my own spruce gum.

There's not much to picking the gum. Look for the hardened resin around scars on the Red Spruce tree. Pry it off and, with a knife blade, scrape the outside to remove any debris. Then begin chewing. At first, the gum is crystalline and shatters. But it soon acquires a certain elasticity, the same as commercially produced chewing gum. This delightful gum is impregnated with the fragrance of the spruce tree. This fragrance, or taste, remains in the gum much longer than does the synthetically produced flavor of commercially made chewing gum.

I sometimes purposely scar young spruce trees on my own woodlot. This ensures a constant supply of spruce gum. Such minor scarring does not harm the trees in the least.

The mature Red Spruce tree usually has irregularly shaped, reddish scales on the bark. The needles, or leaves, are about $1/2$ inch long and are sharp and prickly. Red Spruce trees can grow to 80 feet tall and attain a diameter of 2 feet. The cones are reddish brown, 1 to 2 inches long, and shiny. Look for Red Spruce on the north side of ridges and hills.

A final word on chewing spruce gum: I often become so engrossed in the task that I bite my tongue. Once I bit myself so badly that I probably should have sought medical attention. Instead, I used ice cubes wrapped in a towel to stanch the bleeding. Someone told me, while I was recuperating, that perhaps this injury to my tongue would improve my singing ability. It did not. Persons who are prone to tongue biting should chew with caution.

Willows

(White Willow, *Salix alba;* Black Willow, *Salix nigra;* and other species of willow)

Color plate: Figure 49

Use: Tea, pain reliever. Fast-growing shoots may be stuck in streamside banks to sprout later and provide shade for trout and other fish. Also used in basket weaving, to make emergency snowshoes, and as a dowsing rod to locate sources of underground water.

Range: Throughout New England

Similarity to toxic species: None

Best time: Year-round

Status: Common and abundant

Tools needed: Jackknife

When I acted up as a youth, my grandmother would hand me a jackknife and say "Go cut a switch and bring it to me, Tommy!" The switch would be used to spank me; knowing this, I always chose willow, if there was any at hand. The willow, being supple, didn't cause much pain. Probably my grandma knew this, because I don't remember anything except my youthful pride hurting too badly after a switching.

Again as a child, I remember being told that willow, any willow, was good for trout. If you cut branches in spring and stuck them along the banks, in only a few years willows would spring up and provide shade for the resident trout—and insects living in the trees would fall into the water and provide food for the fish. I have a fond hope that some huge old willows now provide shade for trout, courtesy of my youthful diligence.

Another youthful memory is of my grandpa using a freshly cut willow branch as a dowsing rod. Grandpa found water with ease, and he taught me the skill. And not surprisingly, my favorite medium for a water-dowsing rod is willow.

Once, after reading an old book on woodcraft, I decided to make a set of snowshoes using only basic materials that I could forage. I chose willow because the branches bend so easily without breaking. These were not the best snowshoes, but I decided that had I been in the outback and needed to get out, the homemade snowshoes would have sufficed.

Still, it is the medicinal properties of willow that give this honorable tree a place in this volume. White Willow (and, in my experience, most willows) contains salicin, a profoundly effective pain reliever and inflammation reducer. If the name of this naturally occurring acid sounds familiar, it is because acetylsalicylic acid was synthesized from salicin to make aspirin. Note that today's aspirin is wholly synthetic.

Interestingly, the same unpleasant properties contained in aspirin are present in White Willow bark. While a powerful pain reliever, willow bark tea can also cause painful stomach upsets. Sometimes, though, when I run out of aspirin or other pain relievers and my bad back hurts enough to warrant it, I will gather some fresh willow bark and make a tea rather than get in the car and drive to town for more aspirin.

With a sharp jackknife, whittle about half a teaspoon of the outer and inner bark and chop as finely as possible. Place in a cup, fill with boiling water, and let steep. Drink when cool. This is a powerful drug and will relieve all but the most obstinate pain symptoms.

Here is another little-known use for willow bark. Maine's Penobscot Indians used small, dried chips of willow in their smoking mixtures. The willow turns to charcoal and glows for a long time, keeping the other ingredients lit. And no doubt the smoke contains some of the willow's pain-relieving properties.

Willows are striking in their symmetry. In spring they are among the earliest trees to show some green. The other uses are only icing on an already desirable cake.

— 8 —
Medicinal Plants

Plant medicines are as old as humankind. A decline in the use of plant medicines beginning in the early twentieth century has somewhat reversed itself thanks to the current wave of interest in all things natural. The popularity of alternative medicine has had a positive influence as well.

Commercial interests have jumped upon the "natural" bandwagon, and now patented mixtures of common and not-so-common plants are peddled on television, radio, in magazines, and in health food stores and supermarkets around the country. As someone raised by people who used indigenous medicinal plants as a matter of course, I find it amusing to see processed herbal remedies sold at such high prices. Like the snake oil of old, most of these new herbal medicines contain a laundry list of plants "scientifically" compounded for optimum results.

High on my list of "things not to do" is to buy herbal medicines, especially those that include foreign herbs with names I cannot pronounce. It makes no sense to me to shun modern medical care in favor of what can only be called flimflammery. This is not to say that plant medicines are ineffective; they definitely are not. In fact, lots of plants common to New England provide highly effective remedies for a variety of ailments. And best of all, they are free.

In this chapter I describe my favorite medicinal plants. These are the ones I seek each year. This is necessary because the active shelf life of most herbs is only about one year, so they must be replenished annually.

Three of the more common methods of preparing plant matter for medicinal use are infusions, decoctions, and tinctures, or extracts. Infusions are the quickest and easiest to prepare. An infusion is nothing more than a tea made from different plant parts. The general rule of measurement for infusions is one cup of boiling water poured over one teaspoon of dried plant matter or two teaspoons of chopped fresh plant matter. It is a good idea to begin with these suggested measurements and increase or decrease the plant-to-water ratio as needed. Infusions are best for flowers and leaves.

Next, decoctions are made by simmering plant material in water. This must be done only in a stainless-steel, glass, or enameled metal container. Other kinds of containers may react adversely with the plants. Decoctions are mostly used for the coarser plant parts such as bark, roots, and stems. The ratio of plant to water need not be as precise as in infusions; simply cover the chopped plant matter with water and simmer for half an hour. Above all, do not allow the water to boil. Let cool and strain. Keep the unused portion in the refrigerator.

Tinctures, also called extracts, are the most time-consuming to produce, but plants so preserved remain effective practically indefinitely. To make a tincture, soak plant matter in brandy or vodka. Here again, some herb devotees go overboard, insisting on only "organic" vodka. In fact, whether the grain used to make the vodka was organically grown or not is of no consequence, because the distilling process removes impurities. That's why people wishing for pure water buy the distilled product. Besides, organic vodka costs much more than the conventional product. I use cheap, "rotgut" vodka because it works as well as the ridiculously high-priced stuff and there is essentially no difference between the two.

Basic measurements for making tinctures are four ounces of dried, or eight ounces of fresh, plant matter to one pint of alcohol. Cover the plant matter with the alcohol. Although some people dilute the alcohol with water up to a 50 percent solution, I don't recommend the practice. Let the alcohol-plant mixture sit in a dark, cool place for at least a couple of weeks, then strain through clean muslin into dark-colored bottles.

Some people feel that tinctures made according to the lunar cycle are more effective. I don't think it makes any difference, but for those inclined to add a bit of mysticism to their lives, here is the formula: Using the preceding instructions, make the tincture on a new moon and pour off, or strain, on a full moon.

A final thought on tinctures. They generally are too strong to be taken straight. It is best to mix one teaspoon of tincture to one cup of water.

Valerian
Valeriana officinalis

Color plate: Figure 50

Synonyms: Garden Heliotrope

Use: Tranquilizer, sleep aid

Range: Throughout New England

Similarity to toxic species: The white flower clusters may be confused with some toxic members of the parsley family. Sniffing the bruised root will confirm whether or not the subject is Valerian.

Best time: September through November

Status: Common and abundant

Tools needed: A spading fork or handheld trowel is usually needed to dig the roots.

Valerian is another example of how people can pay for something that they could as easily gather themselves, for free. Valerian is abundant and easily obtained, so it goes against my grain to buy the stuff.

Valerian is a powerful, natural tranquilizer and sleep aid. The root is gathered from fields, waste areas, and rural roadsides in late summer and early fall. The cleaned, dried, and chopped root is used in infusions, to bring on sleep and for its calming effect. A stronger product can be made by using the chopped root in a decoction.

Some herbal remedies work best when taken regularly, over a period of time. Valerian is the opposite. . . . It works within minutes. With no known adverse side effects, it seems odd that more people don't take advantage of Valerian's beneficial properties. There is a catch, however: Valerian root emits a powerful odor. Some liken this scent to old, dirty sweat socks. To me, it smells a bit like the perfume the old-time country women wore to church when I was a kid. The memories it invokes are pleasant enough, so although I can think of things I would rather smell, I am not offended by the odoriferous Valerian root. Interestingly, when in full bloom, Valerian flowers emit a pleasant, sweet aroma, not at all like that of the roots. This alluring scent is most noticeable at night, when it fills the still summer air, charming all who pass by.

An interesting feature of Valerian is that plants growing in poor, gravelly soil are generally more potent than those taken from rich, fertile soil. Some years back I neglected to go to my favorite waste places to gather my winter's supply of Valerian. It was late in the fall and the situation seemed gloomy. Then it occurred to me that I had plenty of the stuff at home. Since Valerian grows to a height of about 4 feet, I had used it in the back of a perennial flower bed as a foil for shorter plants. I dug a few roots; they were huge and, judging from the smell, they would be plenty strong. What a letdown I had when, later that winter, I turned to my store of Valerian for help with insomnia. I made a strong tea, drank it, and returned to bed, certain that the Valerian would soon work its magic. It did not. I went downstairs and took another cup of smelly tea. I may as well have drunk black tea, with caffeine, for all the good the Valerian did me.

Later, I experimented by comparing Valerian root dug from the rough gravel soil of the rural Maine roadsides with Valerian I had purposely cultivated and fed lots of good, rich compost. The wild stuff worked as expected, while the cultivated roots had virtually no effect whatsoever.

Valerian leaves are fernlike, divided, and roughly toothed. The flowers, which are borne in clusters on the top of the stalk, are pure white early on, but later in the season acquire a pinkish hue.

Valerian root is said to be what the Pied Piper of Hamelin used to charm the rats. I used Valerian root as bait in mouse and rat traps and caught exactly nothing. Perhaps my local rodents have more sophisticated taste and will only condescend to visit a trap baited with cheese or peanut butter. Or maybe the story about the Pied Piper is just that . . . a story. Whether Valerian root charms rodents or not, it does soothe weary, jittery people. And that is a good enough reason to dig some next fall, dry it, and store it against a time of need.

Sarsaparilla
Aralia nudicaulis

Color plate: Figures 51 and 52

Use: Tonic

Range: Throughout the region

Similarity to toxic species: None

Best time: May through September

Status: Common and abundant

Tools needed: None

As I've mentioned, one of my favorite hobbies is collecting old-time medicine bottles. And one of my favorite bottles is a tall blue-green beauty with the embossed legend HOODS COMPOUND EXTRACT SARSAPARILLA. Indeed, in the heyday of patent medicines, countless companies produced some kind of sarsaparilla extract or tonic. The lowly sarsaparilla was reputed to cure a host of complaints. Today, people like me use it as a general tonic. Additionally, it tastes good, and if some medicinal benefit can be attributed to taking it, so much the better.

Ironically, more people are familiar with Wild Sarsaparilla because of what it isn't, rather than what it is. A member of the ginseng family, Wild Sarsaparilla closely resembles true ginseng and is frequently confused with that plant. If somebody were to give me a dollar for every time an excited forager showed me the "ginseng" he found, my bank account would swell considerably. Sarsaparilla root is similar to ginseng in that both have ridges on top. And, like ginseng, sarsaparilla root tends to branch, oftentimes resembling the human figure. But where true ginseng leaves are divided palmately—that is, the leafstalks are joined—sarsaparilla leaves are twice divided, with the bottom two leaves joining the stem some distance below the top set of three. Wild Sarsaparilla has tiny white flowers, arranged in a globular shape, atop a long stem. The dark blue berries appear soon after the flowers. Ginseng berries are red.

Sarsaparilla roots are exceedingly long. They run in vast networks through the loose, forest loam. Since Wild Sarsaparilla prefers the mottled shade of mixed-growth woods, and the soil there is usually loose, no tools are needed to harvest the root; simply grab the bottom of a sarsaparilla plant and gently pull, freeing the root with your other hand as it slips free of the earth.

To use sarsaparilla, make a tea. Wash, peel, and chop the root. I like to add a scant handful to a cup of boiling water, but that's quite a strong tea. Others may want to stick to the standard formula for making an infusion.

Sarsaparilla root has a familiar, reassuring fragrance. It reminds me of an old-time general store. Its good taste and pleasing aroma make sarsaparilla a pleasant medicine to take. Try it when that run-down feeling strikes.

Yarrow
Achillea millefolium

Color plate: Figure 53

Synonyms: Thousand-Leaf, Woundwort

Use: Cold, flu, and fever remedy; styptic; toothache remedy; tonic

Range: Throughout the region

Similarity to toxic species: None

Best time: June through October

Status: Common and abundant

Tools needed: None

An old-time formula for a botanical cold and fever medicine consists of equal parts of Yarrow, elderberry blossoms, and Peppermint. While nothing cures a cold, some plants, including Yarrow, can alleviate the symptoms. Of course, Yarrow can be used alone, in an infusion, for colds, flu, and fevers. Either way, it is a fairly effective plant medicine. Yarrow leaves can be chewed for relief of a toothache. They can also be ground, crushed, or slightly chewed and applied directly to minor cuts, as a styptic. And as you might imagine, lots of other virtues are attributed to Yarrow—more than I can conveniently mention here.

The common wild Yarrow, with its creamy white blossoms, is an alien plant, probably brought here purposely for medicinal use. It has since escaped and is common nearly everywhere. Paradoxically, other forms of Yarrow, some in strikingly attractive colors, are cultivated as plants for the perennial flower bed. So while wild Yarrow is ruthlessly pulled and hoed as a weed, its more colorful brethren are admired and pampered.

Pick Yarrow while the plant is in flower. Dry and store in a dark, cool spot. Use the dried leaves and flowers in an infusion. If taken hot, two ounces at a time, it can induce sweating. Lesser amounts, taken cold, have a tonic effect.

Yarrow can grow to 3 feet high. Its distinctive, soft, fernlike leaves clasp the stem. The tiny flowers are borne in dense clusters, atop the stem. Look in waste places, on roadsides, along dirt or gravel drives, and in old, abandoned fields. Yarrow is at home in city lots as well as country dooryards, making it available to everyone, no matter where they might live.

Boneset
Eupatorium perfoliatum

Color plate: Figure 54

Synonyms: Thoroughwort

Use: Fever reducer, laxative

Range: Throughout New England

Similarity to toxic species: None

Best time: July and August

Status: Common

Tools needed: None

"Oh golly, I know what that is," said an elderly participant at one of my slide presentations. "That's Thoroughwort. Father used to take us kids out every year and gather all of it we could find. Then, when we got home, he made us drink as much of it as we could stand. He did this with one child, one day at a time.... We had an outhouse and whoever took the Thoroughwort would spend most of the day there. It cleaned us out real good!"

Boneset, or Thoroughwort, is also a good medicine for fever, as good as any over-the-counter medicine you might buy in the store. Additionally, Boneset is accorded a number of other attributes, as are most of the medicinal herbs.

Even if Boneset had no other redeeming qualities, its physical appearance alone would be sufficient cause for appreciation. Growing as high as 5 feet, Boneset presents a striking picture, with its flat clusters of white flowers atop a stem that apparently grows through its alternating, twinned leaves. If Boneset were not so common, it would surely be prized as a specimen plant by flower gardeners.

Pick Boneset leaves just as the plant goes into flower. The flowers, too, are medicinally active and can be added to the leaves. Look in wet areas, along roadside ditches, in wet woods, and along swamps and bogs. Fortunately for me, the drainage ditch along my driveway is home to lots of Boneset, as well as Skullcap, Jewelweed, and several other useful medicine plants. It's easy for me to determine just when my local Boneset is ready for picking.

The common name, *Boneset,* stems from the plant's use in treating outbreaks of what was called breakbone fever. Apparently, victims of that disease were so tortured that they assumed horribly contorted positions, so as, some worried, to break their bones. Probably no one ever actually suffered broken bones from a fever, except when they fell out of bed, delirious.

Use Boneset in an infusion at the first sign of a fever. It has a bitter taste, which appeals to me. Others may want to add sweetener. And for those gardeners who dare to be different, why not transplant a young Boneset plant to a shady, damp section of the flower bed? Perhaps you will start a new fad!

Heal-All
Prunella vulgaris

Color plate: Figure 55

Synonyms: Self-Heal, Bumblebee Weed

Use: Sore throat remedy, diarrhea remedy

Range: Throughout New England

Similarity to toxic species: None

Best time: July through October

Status: Common and abundant

Tools needed: None

My earliest memory of being treated with wild medicinal plants dates back to when I was seven years old. I had a fever coupled with severe diarrhea. The family doctor paid a house call (that should help date the incident) and gave me something that eventually helped the fever, but had no effect on the diarrhea, which continued for days afterward. I remember my mother being terribly worried about my weight loss. She called my grandpa and asked if he knew of any plant remedy that might save his grandson. That afternoon Grandpa came to the house, a bunch of weeds in hand. He brewed up a terrible-tasting concoction and made me drink it by the waterglass. It stopped the diarrhea cold. Now, as an adult, I harvest Heal-All each fall and dry and store it for winter use.

Heal-All—or Bumblebee Weed, as Grandpa and members of his generation called it (the flowers attract bumblebees)—is one of those unscented members of the mint family. Only its square stem betrays its lineage. Heal-All grows in semishade, along wooded lanes, driveways, and along the edges of fields and woodland openings.

Heal-All should be gathered when in flower and dried for year-round use. Note that the flower spike is never completely covered with blossoms; instead half a dozen at a time may open, giving the thing an unfinished appearance. Anyone who waits for the spike to be fully enveloped in flowers will have a long wait. The paired, ovate leaves have few, if any, teeth and grow opposite each other on the branched stem. Heal-All can grow to about a foot high, but more often reaches only 5 or 6 inches.

Heal-All can be made into a tea, or infusion, for use as a gargle for sore throat. I prefer, though, to simmer the whole plant—leaves, blossoms, and stems—in a decoction until at least half the water has evaporated. The resulting dark liquid can be allowed to cool and gargled to good effect. Also, the stronger decoction is more effective as a diarrhea remedy. Take two ounces at a time, every hour or so, as needed.

All this talk about sore throats and other ailments seems kind of gloomy. It should be remembered that the point of gathering Heal-All, or any of the medicinal plants, is to have the plants on hand if they are needed, but to assume they won't be needed. The fun part is gathering and processing the plants. It's hands-on work in nature, something to look forward to each year, a traditional, seasonal activity. In time, even if the plants are never used medicinally, they become like old, familiar friends, cheering us, adding to our contentment. And that, I feel, is the most valuable aspect of the medicinal plants.

Common Saint-John's-Wort
Hypericum perforatum

Color plate: Figure 56

Use: Medicinal tea, taken for depression

Range: Throughout New England

Similarity to toxic species: None

Best time: August and September

Status: Common and abundant

Tools needed: None

Each fall my neighbor walks the edges of his fields and farm lanes, searching for his winter supply of medicinal plants. One of his favorites is Saint-John's-Wort (also called St. Johnswort). "I take a cup of it on dark days and it cheers me up," he told me. Both the blossoms and the leaves are included in his brew. That this man is cheered from his occasional Saint-John's-Wort tea cannot be disputed. But since Saint-John's-Wort, among other herbs, has a cumulative effect and must be taken over a long period of time, how can a single cup of tea cheer anyone? Moreover, most recipes call for use of the flowers only; my neighbor's tea may therefore be weaker than it might be if only the blossoms were used. What gives here?

Consider when Saint-John's-Wort is ready for picking. It is at its peak of perfection in late summer and early fall, that glorious, New England mini season that encompasses the best of two worlds: bright, balmy days and cool, crisp nights. A more cheerful time of year cannot be imagined. Next, picking medicinal plants is just plain fun. And it's reassuring to know that in a single day it's possible to harvest a season's supply of beneficial plants. In short, everything about the medicinal plant harvest is positive and upbeat. Drinking a cup of Saint-John's-Wort tea revives all these pleasant thoughts. So now it's easy to understand how my neighbor is cheered every time he downs a cup of tea.

Saint-John's-Wort is not only a useful medicinal plant but also a pretty wildflower with some attractive characteristics. The botanical name for its species, *perforatum*, discloses an interesting physical property: The leaves are dotted with little round holes. Lacking very young eyes, it is necessary to use a handheld magnifier to fully appreciate these holes or, more accurately stated, oil pockets. Although nobody else describes them this way, I think the pockets look much like moon-style craters, with a small berm on the surface. Probably this is a product of an overly active imagination, aided and abetted by the view "through the looking-glass."

Saint-John's-Wort leaves are paddle shaped and opposite, small in comparison to the size of the plant. The bright yellow flowers have five petals with bristly stamens. Although the plant can grow to about 18 inches tall, it can also be recumbent. There is one such vining specimen in the rock garden in front of my cottage.

Now to the commercial hype about Saint-John's-Wort. This plant, along with Purple Coneflower *(Echinacea purpurea)*, is responsible for making untold millions of dollars for various companies, each claiming that its product is superior to other over-the-counter herbal remedies. The logic here is that the power of the commercial product is somehow controlled or manipulated into a standard strength. Someone once told me that it would be impossible for me, or anyone else, to get the same benefit from the wild Saint-John's-Wort growing literally everywhere as can be realized from the commercial product. To that, I can say only that the Greeks had a word for such nonsense . . . *baloney!* All right, maybe it wasn't the Greeks who said that, but the point is that Saint-John's-Wort is Saint-John's-Wort, no matter how you slice it. Here's my advice for those who don't want to spend a small fortune for the commercially available stuff.

Pick the plant in blossom. Try to get more flowers than leaves, but don't worry about the ratio of each, as long as the stems are discarded. Dry the plant and, when dry, rub it between your palms. Store it in a closed jar or bag and use a teaspoon in a cup of tea to cheer the spirits. Herbalists will recommend that the tea be taken daily, on an ongoing basis, for the relief of depression. I cannot say if this works or not, since I've never been truly depressed. But the occasional cup is enough to lift my spirits, and many experts say that regular use of Saint-John's-Wort does combat true depression. In the end, I would harvest, dry, and use my own herb for steady use, rather than relying upon the commercially available stuff.

There is a side effect. Saint-John's-Wort can cause photosensitivity.

Animals can suffer skin burns after grazing on the plant. Fair-skinned people may be well advised to refrain from ingesting more than the occasional cup of Saint-John's-Wort tea. And don't forget the sunblock!

Canada Goldenrod
Solidago canadensis

Color plate: Figure 57

Synonyms: Goldenrod

Use: Leaf tea for fever and gas; blossoms chewed for sore throat

Range: Throughout the region

Similarity to toxic species: None

Best time: August and September

Status: Despised weed, common and widespread

Tools needed: None

Canada Goldenrod is widespread throughout the Northeast. It is easy to distinguish Canada Goldenrod from other goldenrod species by the leaves. They are sharply toothed and have a prominent center vein with two parallel, curved outer veins. The bright yellow blossoms are borne on horizontal plumes, with the exception of the very tip, which is more or less a continuation of the main stalk of the plant.

Once, blooming goldenrod saddened me because it signaled the end of summer. That was before I recognized that blooming plants represent separate seasons, special times on nature's calendar. Goldenrod, for instance, blooms at the same time as Saint-John's-Wort, Butter-and-Eggs, Sow Thistles, and a host of other wild plants having yellow blossoms. Indeed, because so many plants with yellow blossoms are at their peak now, this might rightly be called "the yellow season." At least that's how I define it. The yellow season should be appreciated for what it is, a short but glorious page on the grand list of annual events.

Watery eyes, runny noses, hacking and wheezing . . . allergy season happens every fall. Most allergy sufferers blame goldenrod for these unpleasant symptoms. Admittedly, goldenrod can cause allergic reactions in some individuals, but the bulk of allergy sufferers are victims of ragweed pollen, not goldenrod pollen. No matter, though. People will continue to blame goldenrod for their misery despite evidence to the contrary. Thus, I have become a goldenrod apologist.

Because goldenrod gets such bad press, I make an example of it as a "good weed," a beautiful and useful, if largely unappreciated plant. So when the Canada Goldenrod (the most common species in our area) comes into bloom, I pick the most symmetrically shaped blooming ends and put them in a vase, along with some orange hawkweed, for contrast. And because the goldenrods bloom so late in the year, it is possible to add them to bouquets of blue- and magenta-colored New England Asters. Such visually appealing combinations of color and style are hallmarks of late summer in New England.

Even people who don't suffer unduly from sensitivity to ragweed pollen can experience some discomfort during the allergy season. Fortunately, Canada Goldenrod, rather than being responsible for people's misery, is ready to step into the gap, especially when scratchy or sore throats make life miserable. When this happens, I chew on fresh blossoms of Canada Goldenrod. The spicy taste alone would be reason enough to partake, but the fact is, the stuff alleviates minor sore throat discomfort. Just pick and chew—so simple yet so effective. Score another point in goldenrod's favor.

Goldenrod leaf tea is a pleasant beverage, but more than that, an infusion of leaves and blossoms can dispel stomach gas. It also encourages sweating, which can help alleviate fever symptoms. Add yet another mark in favor of goldenrod.

Clearly, given that Canada Goldenrod has far more benefits than deficits, it is time for foragers to become patrons of this handsome yet maligned plant of the fields, hedgerows, and waste places.

Goldthread
Coptis groenlandica

Color plate: Figure 58

Synonyms: Canker Root

Use: A bitter, appetite-stimulating tonic; a tincture gargled for mouth sores or sore throat; a tea used for colds; a root chewed for canker sores

Range: Throughout New England

Similarity to toxic species: None

Best time: Whenever the ground is not frozen

Status: Common and abundant

Tools needed: None

Goldthread grows in lush colonies on the forest floor, thriving in the partial shade and cool, damp conditions afforded by a mixed-growth canopy. Goldthread is also common in sphagnum bogs. As with so many common woodland plants, almost everybody has seen Goldthread, but few have ever taken time to examine it carefully, and fewer still can accurately identify the plant.

As the common name implies, the roots of Goldthread are long, thin, and of a bright yellow color. Each Goldthread plant has a great mass of roots, most of which grow laterally only an inch or two beneath the surface. The shiny evergreen leaves have coarse teeth and grow in groups of three, much like strawberry leaves. The pretty white flowers have five sepals and five petals.

Harvesting Goldthread roots is a cinch. Goldthread always grows on loose ground, and all the forager need do is, using the bare fingers, lift the top layer of forest litter or sphagnum moss to expose the vast network of brilliant yellow roots. Picking the individual roots is somewhat tedious, but ten minutes of effort can produce a great quantity.

The easiest way to use Goldthread is to pick a root, brush it clean, and chew on it. This applies the medicine directly to the mouth and is an efficient way to treat any sores of the mouth or gums. The next, and perhaps the most interesting, way to use Goldthread root is as a bitter tonic. The reasons for taking bitters are given in the chapter on Ground Ivy (see page 155) and needn't be repeated here, except to say that if you appreciate the bitter digestive tonic made from Ground Ivy, you will probably enjoy the Goldthread product even more. It has a clean, sharp taste, one that I find both pleasant and stimulating.

To make the tonic, chop the fresh roots finely and use one teaspoon chopped root to one cup of boiling water. These proportions may be modified according to taste. Let it steep for half an hour before straining. Use one teaspoon of the tonic before meals. It can also be used as a gargle for sore throats and hoarseness. Refrigerate unused portions.

Finally, a Goldthread tincture is one of the more effective and reliable sore throat medicines. Besides using it myself, I have given this product to ailing friends; without exception, they have gained some amount of relief. Goldthread is made into a tincture for use in winter, when the ground is frozen and the fresh root cannot be obtained.

I sometimes use the tincture undiluted, as a gargle for sore throats. This goes against the rule that tinctures should never be taken straight. The idea, though, is not to swallow the stuff, but to swish it around in the throat and then spit it out. I mention this method only because it works for me; I don't recommend that anyone ever use any tincture undiluted.

Given Goldthread's effectiveness as a medicine, its virtues as a digestive aid, and its abundance and easy availability, it should rank high on every forager's list of medicinal plants.

Spotted Joe-Pye Weed
Eupatorium maculatum

Color plate: Figure 59

Synonyms: Smokeweed

Use: The leaf tea is a cold and flu remedy.

Range: Throughout New England

Similarity to toxic species: None

Best time: August

Status: Common and abundant

Tools needed: None

"It won't be long now. The Joe-Pye Weed is already blooming," a friend once told me. His observation was really a comment that the summer was fast drawing to a close. Joe-Pye Weed blooms in August, a prelude to the approaching autumn.

Spotted Joe-Pye Weed is abundant in northern New England. It grows to about 4 feet tall. The cupped, lance-shaped leaves are coarsely toothed and surround the stem in whorls of four or five leaves each. The flower clusters are borne on top of the plant and are pink to red in color. Spotted Joe-Pye Weed prefers damp ground, growing in roadside ditches and along streamsides. Several other joe-pye weeds are found in New England, namely Sweet Joe-Pye Weed, *E. purpureum* (so named because the crushed flowers emit a vanillalike scent), and Joe-Pye Weed, *E. dubium*. Both these are more common in southern New England.

Spotted Joe-Pye Weed is a striking plant, and innovative gardeners use it as a background plant in perennial beds. Medicinally, the various joe-pye weeds are similar in action to Boneset. I use the two interchangeably. Traditionally, it is the roots that are used medicinally, but I use the leaves in an infusion and find they work just fine. Although a host of other medicinal claims are made for Spotted Joe-Pye Weed, I prefer to use it only for the common cold, flu, and fever.

Mugwort

Artemisia vulgaris

Color plate: Figures 60 and 61

Use: The leaves are poulticed for rheumatism, or steeped in tea for a digestive tonic and for cold and fever relief.

Range: Throughout New England

Similarity to toxic species: Mugwort closely resembles Wormwood, *A. absinthium,* which contains thujone, a toxin.

Best time: August and September

Status: Common and abundant

Tools needed: None

The person who coined the term *weed* must have been thinking of Mugwort. It is virtually everywhere. Present in every vacant lot, railroad siding, landfill, and waste area, Mugwort is familiar to anyone who ever stepped outside. Even in the early season, Mugwort looks half dead and scruffy, because the bottom leaves dry, curl, turn yellow, and then brown. Who would ever guess this unassuming, omnipresent weed has considerable medicinal value?

Mugwort leaves are deeply cut, light green on top and silvery colored on the bottom. When a stiff wind turns the leaves up, the plant assumes a ghostly shade of silver. The tiny, fuzzy, yellowish brown "flowers" grow in bunches at the end of the stem. The crushed leaves and flowers emit a pungent aroma.

Mugwort is another plant with a plethora of virtues attached to it. One herbal guide describes it as helpful in cases of rheumatism, gout, kidney and bladder trouble, female trouble (whatever that may be), and suppressed menstruation. This same booklet fails to indicate Mugwort's use as a digestive tonic, or its use against the common cold and accompanying fever. Ironically, the latter two uses are the only ones I can personally recommend.

Once, by way of experimentation, I took Mugwort somewhat regularly to see if it might help my rheumatism. It didn't. But it did make me feel generally good, probably because it aided my digestion. And while taking it, I didn't get a cold. If all wild-plant medicines were so effective, the doctor would go broke.

The way to pick Mugwort is to slide your hand along the stem, pulling bunches of leaves. There is no need to break the stem. Dried Mugwort leaves are handy to have in the medicine cabinet in fall and winter, during the cold and flu season. An aromatic cup of Mugwort tea tickles the senses, warms the soul, and fights cold symptoms all at the same time.

9

The Waste Places

Lots of useful plants grow in waste places—areas where the ground is poor, wet, perhaps a trifle too acid, rocky, windy, or otherwise unacceptable to most cultivated plants. These spots are everywhere: behind someone's house in town, along the country dweller's driveway. They may include the unmowed edge of a community baseball field or the weedy bank where garden refuse and grass clippings are unceremoniously dumped.

No matter where they're found, in towns, the city, or the open countryside, waste places provide a unique habitat for dozens of edible and medicinal plants. And therein lies a twisted irony: the idea that anyplace that hosts such valuable plants should be called a "waste" place.

Japanese Knotweed
Polygonum cuspidatum

Color plate: Figures 62 and 63

Synonyms: Bamboo

Use: Cooked vegetable, pie ingredient, stewed vegetable

Range: Throughout New England

Similarity to toxic species: None

Best time: April and May; into early June in the north

Status: Common. Despised as an invasive weed

Tools needed: None

Most homeowners who have knotweed growing on their property hate the stuff. Japanese Knotweed is number one on lists of invasive plants to avoid. Countless hours of toil are wasted in trying to eradicate Japanese Knotweed, and untold gallons of toxic poisons are introduced into the environment in a misplaced effort to kill the plant. Personally, I prefer to eat it. Knotweed is truly a food for the nonconformist.

Most people think Japanese Knotweed is a form of bamboo. It is not, nor is it even distantly related to the bamboos. It's in the buckwheat family, related to another edible plant, Lady's Thumb. Knotweed is confused with bamboo because the stem has similar-looking nodes. It isn't necessary to quote the scientific name of this shrublike weed when dealing with it, but it would be good to refer to it by its proper common name, Japanese Knotweed.

Japanese Knotweed was introduced to this country in the Victorian era as an ornamental. It does have a rather attractive style, but the flowers, which were the main drawing card back then, are too small and their whitish green color too drab to elicit much praise now. Since then knotweed has spread across the country, although never far from the original plantings. Search any old homestead, or look around any old rock foundation. Chances are, two plants will be growing nearby—a huge, ancient lilac bush and a great stand of Japanese Knotweed. Knotweed is, I feel, unjustly damned as an invader.

In spring, when the blackflies are at their gnawing, swarming worst, Japanese Knotweed sends up its young shoots. This is the time to pick the stuff, before the plant grows higher than a few feet. The way to tell if a knotweed shoot is still tender, even if it is fairly tall, is to bend the very end. The last 6 or 8 inches should snap easily, with a hollow, popping sound. Two people picking at once make a sound like popcorn popping. Since knotweed grows in vast colonies (in many instances these colonies are so huge because they are more than a hundred years old), it's easy to snap off half a bushel in no time.

It is not necessary to remove the undeveloped leaves at the tip of the shoot, although any larger leaves, growing from the sheaths on the nodes, should be removed. The easiest, and my favorite, way to prepare knotweed is to put only a little water in a frying pan, get the water to simmering, and add the rinsed knotweed shoots. These are done when they turn light green and are droopy. Don't overcook, or they will turn to mush. Three to five minutes' cooking time is usually plenty. Treat the knotweed "spears" the same as asparagus spears—that is, serve hot with salt, pepper, and butter. Don't expect knotweed to taste like asparagus, though. The taste of the steamed shoots defies description. Most people like it and some, like me, love it. Even though numbers of other tasty, plentiful wild foods are available at the same time as knotweed, I always make it a point to enjoy a stretch of "knotweed madness," a week or so during which I eat steamed knotweed shoots every day. That usually is enough to hold me until the knotweed is ready the following year.

Here's an intriguing thought. Invite the neighbors—preferably neighbors who have spent their weekend digging and cursing the Japanese Knotweed on the edge of their lawn—to dinner. Make a nice spread, with wine, candles, and lots of pretty appetizers before the meal. As the featured vegetable, serve steamed Japanese Knotweed shoots, but don't tell your guests what it is. Only reveal the identity of this delicious "mystery" vegetable after the commensurate amount of pleading and prodding. Oh, the devious mind of the hard-core forager!

Knotweed can be stewed, the same as rhubarb. Add sugar to taste while stewing. This process is similar to the one used in making Wild Cranberry sauce. Use only a little water and let the product simmer for about ten minutes while stirring in sugar and sampling frequently. Let cool and refrigerate. Serve chilled, topped with whipped cream. Or the stewed knotweed can be used as a pie filling or frozen for future use.

Knotweed grows to about 10 feet high. The olive-drab stems are smooth, shiny, and hollow. They are often mottled with red spots, as if somebody splashed paint on them. The node joints are covered with a papery membrane, much like knotweed's relative, Lady's Thumb. The leaves are wide, roundly pointed, and lack teeth. The flowers, which bloom in late summer, are borne on long, thin stalks.

While Japanese Knotweed is best harvested in mid- to late spring, it can be located at any time of the year; look for the brown, dried, bamboolike stalks from the previous year's crop.

Jewelweed
Impatiens capensis

Color plate: Figure 64

Synonyms: Spotted Touch-Me-Not

Use: Cooked green; Poison Ivy and rash remedy

Range: Everywhere in New England, especially in shady, moist places, and on roadsides

Similarity to toxic species: None

Best time: April and May

Status: Common and abundant

Tools needed: None

Jewelweed is a crossover plant: It is eminently edible, yet has great medicinal value. Jewelweed is among the earliest fresh green plants available in New England. In early spring, as soon as wood frogs began their sporadic croaking in the wet areas, I search for Jewelweed seedlings. These, although small, can be gathered in great handfuls. At this point, it is the seed leaves, or cotyledons, along with the weak, succulent stalks, that are eaten. A few weeks later the plant takes on something like its adult appearance, although it is still only 6 inches high.

The immature Jewelweed shoots should be washed in a colander and trimmed of their roots, if any remain attached. Then, drop a few handfuls into a slight amount of boiling water or cook in a vegetable steamer. Five minutes is more than enough time to cook the young Jewelweed shoots. Drain and serve with a pat of butter and season to taste. The older plants, up to 12 inches tall, are edible too, but the stems become tough; it is best to use only the leaves and tender tips now. Cooking takes a bit longer as well.

Though Jewelweed is a superb vegetable, it is more widely known for its healing qualities. Indeed, many people who are familiar with the plant as a medicinal herb are surprised to learn that it is equally as useful on the table.

Jewelweed is most useful as a curative when it is mature, or nearly so. The plants grow in dense colonies along country roads, ditches, and driveways. Interestingly, the ground under Jewelweed plants is always moist, even on the hottest days of summer. The smooth, lightly ribbed leaves are more or less spear shaped, the succulent stems are partially translucent, and the orange, trumpet-shaped blossoms hang from a thin, flexible stem. The ripe seedpods are pressure-sensitive and forcibly eject their cargo of seeds when touched. Children (including big kids, like me) are fond of squeezing the seedpods and watching the seeds, with their clockspring-shaped triggers, spew forth. It's great fun to gently pick only the largest seedpods; when a handful is gathered (this is hard to do without them bursting prematurely), touch one and watch it set off a chain reaction.

Back to Jewelweed's medicinal value. For the itch of Poison Ivy, just crush the juicy stems and rub on the affected area. For immediate protection in the field, when Poison Ivy is accidentally encountered, rub on Jewelweed. The rash probably won't develop, as long as the body part that touched the poison ivy is washed with soap and water later on.

Poison Ivy is not the only itch that Jewelweed treats. Heat rash, bug bites, and a host of other complaints are all nullified by a poultice of crushed Jewelweed stems and leaves.

Jewelweed's curative powers can be preserved for off-season use, too. Gather an armload of stems and leaves, and simmer in a large saucepan, or clam and lobster steamer, until the water is reduced by half and has turned a deep, dark brown. Lift out and discard the spent Jewelweed, and allow the juice to cool. As soon as it's cool, pour into ice cube trays and freeze. After the cubes are frozen, I like to remove them from the trays and put them in a plastic bag, which I keep in the freezer for immediate use at any time. It sometimes helps itchy, dry skin to drop a few Jewelweed cubes in the bath water. Or place a cube in a washcloth and gently wipe the itchy skin. The list of ills that might be cured by Jewelweed juice is long.

I'm fond of asking guests if they want to see my impatiens bed. If they say yes, I walk them over alongside my gravel driveway to a thick stand of Jewelweed. When I am finally convinced that they have puzzled over this apparent contradiction for long enough, I explain that Jewelweed *is* an impatiens, albeit a wild variety.

My fondness for the physical properties of Jewelweed is based upon a practical appreciation of nature. Jewelweed is so called because water beads up on the "unwettable" leaves; when the sun hits them, the little droplets gleam like so many jewels. Sunrise on a still, summer morning is my favorite time of day to poke about outside and watch the Jewelweed glisten in the morning light.

Jewelweed is an exemplar of the various wildlings that offer beauty of form, color, and texture in addition to other, more practical uses. If we can only get past the "wildness" of some of these useful plants, we will appreciate them as fully as we do the cultivated varieties that we pay so much good money to pamper.

Common Milkweed
Asclepias syriaca

Color plate: Figures 65 and 66

Use: Milkweed provides several kinds of cooked vegetables.

Range: Throughout New England

Similarity to toxic species: Butterfly Weed, *A. tuberosa*, is a toxic member of the milkweed family. Butterfly Weed has orange flowers, the stem does not exude a milky latex when broken (Common Milkweed does), and the seedpods are thinner than those of Common Milkweed. Also, although very young Common Milkweed shoots are edible, it is advisable not to pick them on account of their similarity to young members of the toxic dogbane family, the genus *Apocynum*.

Best time: June for tender tips, July for the blossoms and seedpods

Status: Common and abundant

Tools needed: Gloves protect the hands from the sticky, latexlike sap.

Milkweed leaves are nearly oblong, except they are roundly pointed at the tip. They grow opposite each other. All parts of the plant exude a sticky, milky substance when broken. The seedpods are 2 inches or more long, green, and warty.

An old woman, a friend of the family, first enlightened me as to the edible qualities of Common Milkweed. This lady, who would be well over a hundred years old now if she were alive, told me that as a youngster, her family relished the young milkweed tips, picking only the four-leaved top of the young plant. These they ate boiled, after the manner of string beans or cabbage. It took me only as long as the short drive to the nearest milkweed patch to sample this product. They were excellent.

People who would never dream of eating it use Common Milkweed. The seedpods are routinely gathered and dried by those who make dried flower arrangements. Sometimes the warty pods are sprayed with gold enamel. And every child who witnesses the wind carrying the fluffy seeds from the opened seedpod feels compelled to help the process by gathering bunches of the seedpods and scattering their contents to the prevailing wind.

Back to Common Milkweed's edibility. As mentioned earlier, when the plant is young, the tips, with their four leaves, are edible. Here's what to look for. Looking down at the plant, two small leaves will be seen directly opposite each other, and two more leaves, this time smaller, will be seen, again opposite each other, half a turn removed. The leaf configuration, then, will resemble a plus (+) sign. Snip these leaves with thumb and forefinger. Steam for about fifteen minutes and serve with butter, salt, and pepper. Some people find Common Milkweed bitter to the taste and so cook it in two waters. This process is described in the chapter on Marsh Marigolds (see page 33).

Later, when the plant blossoms, the globular clusters of unopened flower buds offer yet another food product. These buds are good until the flowers begin to open. Although the flowers are tinged with lavender, they turn green when boiled for at least 10 minutes. Use two waters if desired. These are so well liked by guests at my wild-food luncheons that I regularly freeze quantities of them in order to assure a steady supply, even out of season. The texture of the cooked buds somewhat resembles broccoli, although the taste is completely different.

Finally, the seedpods, when young and firm, make an unusual and delicious food. When cooked, the husk becomes soft and tender and the silken seeds congeal. The texture and taste of the pods makes them a personal favorite of mine, and I always freeze some for winter use. Cook the pods until tender, in two waters, if desired.

It is interesting to note that the milky latex sap is toxic, but cooking destroys the toxins. Never consume the raw sap.

Great Burdock
Arctium lappa

Color plate: Figure 67

Synonyms: Burdock

Use: Cooked vegetable

Range: Throughout New England

Similarity to toxic species: None

Best time: Young leaves in April and early May; stalks in June and July

Status: Despised as an invasive weed

Tools needed: None

Dog owners know all too well the difficulty of removing the burrs (the burrs contain the seeds) of Great Burdock and Common Burdock, *A. minus*, from their pet's coat. The burrs also pose a hazard for humans who wear wool shirts or pants; the individual "hooks" found in the burrs can only be removed through tedious, painstaking effort. Who would ever think this coarse plant was not only edible, but tasty too?

Burdock provides several food products. The first, and the easiest to deal with, are the young leaves. These can be harvested in very early spring, as soon as the top layer of ground thaws. The leaves are egg shaped and extremely wavy, or crinkled on the margins. When these are from 2 to 3 inches long, they make a good boiling green. Boil for at least fifteen minutes to render the leaves tender. Some prefer to cook burdock leaves in two waters. I use only one, but sometimes add a small pinch of baking soda to tenderize the leaves and to remove any inherent bitterness. Burdock leaves don't lose much bulk in cooking, so what you begin with is pretty much what you end with, a true Yankee bargain if ever there was one. Look on south-facing slopes of gravel banks and other rough, waste places for the first burdock leaves of the season.

The remaining uses of burdock involve considerable work and in my view, are not worth the effort. Nevertheless, they deserve mention because others may find the process more rewarding. First, the roots of the first-year plants (burdock is biennial) are edible. The work begins with digging the long taproots. Note that they do not give up without a fight. Then they must be peeled and cooked in two waters for up to half an hour before being served as a root vegetable.

Finally, the inner core of the young leafstalks and flower stalks is edible, either raw or cooked, but the process of removing the outside rind is tedious. The cores are cooked as per the process used for the roots.

Great Burdock hardly needs describing. The mature plant somewhat resembles rhubarb, in that the leaves are roughly the same size. The round burrs are brown and prickly; the stalks of the basal leaves have a slight groove. The plant grows more than 8 feet high.

Burdock roots are relished in Japan, so don't let my lack of interest in this very available wild food tarnish your desire to try them. Even so, I would stick to the young leaves, one of the first wild edibles of the new season.

Orpine
Sedum purpureum

Color plate: Figure 68

Synonyms: Live-Forever

Use: Trail nibble, salad ingredient, cooked vegetable

Range: Throughout New England

Similarity to toxic species: None

Best time: April and May

Status: Common and abundant

Tools needed: A hand trowel helps dislodge the tubers.

Rural youngsters know this plant not for its culinary properties, but because it is fun to separate the edges of the fleshy leaves, blow on the seam, and make an ersatz balloon, which can later be popped between the palms.

Adults may see some similarity between a common rock garden plant, Autumn Joy Sedum, and common Orpine. The resemblance is more than superficial, since both belong to the same genus.

The flavor of the young leaves is mild, yet pronounced. Once, while on an early-season fishing trip, the trout refused to bite but the field that bounded the stream was filled with young Orpine, the leaves at just the perfect stage for munching. I went home fishless but full, from eating a huge quantity of Orpine leaves.

Around the time the Ostrich Fern fiddleheads are ripe, which in my part of New England is around the first week of May, the Orpine tubers are ready. Really, the tubers are good as soon as they can be located in spring, but I like to combine fiddleheading with tuber picking. And although a trowel is sometimes needed to remove the abundant tubers from the ground, Orpine's habit of growing on gravel banks ensures that the ground is usually loose and the plant—roots, tubers, and all—can be uprooted without any mechanical assistance.

Each plant hosts a large bunch of elongated tubers. These grow laterally in the ground, with tubers branching out in all directions. Select the largest from each group and return the rest to the soil to propagate another clump of Orpine.

At home, rinse all sand and gravel from the tubers and boil for fifteen to twenty minutes. Serve with butter, salt, and pepper. These go nicely with a dish of boiled Ostrich Fern fiddleheads, supplying the "potato" part of the meal. A few fresh trout complement the feast nicely, but more plebeian sources of protein may be substituted if necessary. For a finishing touch, serve a salad of Common Blue Violet leaves and blossoms, some chopped Clintonia leaves, and a few chopped young Orpine leaves. Soft music and candlelight are optional.

Orpine leaves are smooth and succulent, that is, fat and fleshy. They are light green, have smooth, rough teeth, and grow alternately on the stem, in a whorl. The tuberous roots resemble thin parsnips, and seldom reach more than 2 inches long.

Evening Primrose
Oenothera biennis

Color plate: Figures 69, 70, and 71

Use: Serve root and young leaves as a cooked vegetable.

Range: Throughout New England

Similarity to toxic species: None

Best time: Very early spring, March and early April

Status: Common and abundant

Tools needed: A hand trowel is useful to dislodge the roots.

The staccato croak of the wood frog rings through my mind every time Evening Primrose is mentioned. The two go together, because when the first wood frog of the season (wood frogs begin their chorus even earlier than spring peepers) utters its first, raspy note, it is time to dig Evening Primrose roots.

The Evening Primrose is biennial, and it is the first year's taproot that foragers seek in early spring. Locate these by first seeking the tall, woody stalks left over from the previous year. The dried seedpods, or capsules, on the old plants are cylindrical in shape; on the end they are reflexed, or scalloped, evidence of the manner in which the seeds were dispersed. In order to locate the new plants, stand near the old plant and consider the prevailing wind. . . . It is in this direction that the seeds will have fallen, and it is here that the basal rosettes of the young plants will be found.

The young leaves lie flat on the ground, radiating from a central point. They are long and slender, with a pinkish midrib, and are tinged with red on the ends. Later, when spring arrives in earnest, these leaves will stand up and the plant will send forth the young shoot. The time to pick the leaves as a boiling green is when they are still flat on the ground. This season is brief; during a warm spell, the plant can become too far gone in only a few days.

Some recommend eating the leaves in a salad, but this doesn't agree with my taste. My preferred use is to cook them for only about five minutes and serve with the usual butter, salt, and pepper. Other foragers cook the young leaves in two changes of water. If they are harvested after they stand erect, this is probably a good idea. I am content to use them only during their peak period, before such treatment is necessary. Then they are sweet and mild.

The roots, too, are at their best while the leaves are spread flat upon the ground. These can be surprisingly large, as large as the average supermarket carrot. They are creamy white in color, with a top that is approximately the same shade of red as the breast on a rose-breasted grosbeak. Pick as many of the roots as time will permit (don't worry about hurting the stand; they won't be any good next year anyway), take them home, and wash them. Next, they need to be peeled or scrubbed. Here's a neat trick—something that saves time and energy when preparing not only Evening Primrose roots, but lots of other root veggies as well: Hold the root under running water and scrub with a clean copper-pot scrubber. This is vastly easier than using a knife or potato peeler.

Next, half-fill a frying pan with water and bring the water to a low boil. If the roots are very small, add them whole. If they are medium or large, slice them lengthwise in two or four pieces. Cook for at least ten minutes. Drain and serve with butter, salt, and pepper. The taste is different from any other root vegetable; it is impossible for me to adequately describe it, except to say that it is sweet, mild, and very pleasant.

The most important thing to remember about Evening Primroses is that it is never too early in the season for them.... They would be good if taken from under the snow, if they could be located then.

Pineapple Weed
Matricaria matricarioides

Color plate: Figures 72 and 73

Use: Tea

Range: Throughout New England

Similarity to toxic species: None

Best time: June through October

Status: Common and abundant

Tools needed: None

During a plant walk, I once pointed to some Pineapple Weed and asked a lady if she knew what it was. "Sure," she replied. "It's chamomile." She had unwittingly used Pineapple Weed for the same purpose as chamomile: for colds and as an aid to relaxation. The Pineapple Weed apparently worked, but whether this was from its inherent medicinal properties or the power of wishful thinking is hard to determine.

The chamomile lady was correct in one thing. Pineapple Weed is properly utilized as the single ingredient in a mellow, pineapple-scented, golden tea. But is that all this diminutive plant is good for? Hardly! I like to pick the crumbly flower heads, slightly crush them, and place them in my shirt pocket as I walk along. The pineapple scent is not pervasive, but it is enough to lift the spirits and brighten the day. Sometimes I chew on the flower heads, just enough to release the delightful pineapple flavor.

Pick as many of the greenish yellow flower heads as patience will allow. Use a teaspoon of dried (the flower heads dry easily for year-round use), or two teaspoons of the fresh product. Cover with boiling water and let them steep for up to five minutes. Honey may be added, but I recommend sampling the tea as is first.

Pineapple Weed grows abundantly along gravel paths, roads, and on gravelly lots. It prefers full sun, but can take partial shade. It rarely gets much over a foot tall—usually it is only 5 or 6 inches high. The feathery leaves resemble those of chamomile, but the flower heads are tightly packed and lack chamomile's white petals. The easiest way to identify this plant is to crush the flower head and sniff it. If it doesn't smell like pineapple, it is the wrong plant.

Here is a pleasant, unassuming little plant that offers a sweet fragrance and a satisfying tea. What more could anyone ask of a plant?

Common Plantain
Plantago major

Color plate: Figure 74

Synonyms: Plantain

Use: Cooked vegetable, salad ingredient

Range: Throughout New England

Similarity to toxic species: None

Best time: April and May are best, but new leaves can be harvested throughout the growing season.

Status: Common and abundant

Tools needed: None

Is there anyone who has not encountered Common Plantain? What child has not delighted in "shooting" the seeds from the long, thin seed stalk? This plant thrives in virtually every dooryard in the nation. And yet few people recognize its value and worth.

The basal leaves are broad, deeply veined, rounded at the ends, and have wavy margins. The seed heads stand taller than the leaves, which tend to stay close to the ground. The leafstalk has a trough, or groove.

This is a multifaceted plant. First, Common Plantain has some medicinal properties that everyone should be familiar with. Crushed, the leaves and stalks are useful in soothing the sting of rash, insect bites, sunburn, and mild burns. In fact, plantain can effectively replace calamine lotion—and it doesn't leave that pasty residue, either. Herbalists use Common Plantain in an infusion to treat sore throats and coughs. Finally, a decoction of the whole plant is reputed to combat dandruff.

My main interest in plantain, though, is as a food source. The young leaves are excellent when steamed or boiled for only four or five minutes. Be sure to pick leaves that are no longer than 2 inches, or they will be tough and stringy. While the leaves are best in spring, they can be culled from the adult plants at any time of year because plantain constantly renews itself.

Plantain was widely used by the colonists, but in the intervening years commercially produced medicine and cultivated vegetables have superseded it. Perhaps now, this lowly dooryard weed will receive some of the praise it so richly deserves.

Wild Raspberries and Blackberries
Rubus spp.

Color plate: Figure 75

Use: Trail nibble, jam, fruit dessert, tea (leaves), wine

Range: Throughout New England

Similarity to toxic species: None

Best time: July through September

Status: Common and abundant

Tools needed: None

Wild raspberries are generally sweeter and smaller than the cultivated variety. Other than that, they are much the same. Wild blackberries are considerably larger than wild raspberries and fill the collecting pail in a shorter time. Both berries are pioneer plants, filling the void when land is clear-cut or burned over.

In years past my fondness for wild raspberries led me to an old farmstead, far off the road, in a mountainous area of Maine. The berries here were larger than most, because they grew in patches in the middle of large, overgrown fields. Human foragers were not aware of the annual bounty, but the local bears were well informed. They wallowed in the bramble patches, crushing the vines and wreaking havoc in general. Once, a local resident told me that a bear had roused him out of a sound sleep in the wee hours of the morning. It seemed that the animal had gorged itself on raspberries and somehow, the berries had fermented, making the bruin drunk. It staggered, groaned, fell down, and crashed into the side of the man's house before stumbling off into the night. To the uninitiated, this may sound like a fanciful tale. But since it is known that ruffed grouse frequently become soused when feeding on apples, why shouldn't the same apply to bears?

Wild raspberry leaves make a pleasant, if somewhat astringent, tea. This tea can be used for mild cases of diarrhea. For the strongest medicine, pick the leaves while the plant is in flower. Either use them fresh or dry the leaves completely; wilting makes them toxic, but the toxin disappears when the leaf is dry. It is easy to pick lots of leaves, dry them, and store them in a closed container for winter use. Blackberry brandy is also used to control diarrhea. Blackberry brandy can be made at home by mixing the juice (extract this either by simmering the berries in a slight amount of water or by running them through a food mill) with vodka and sugar. Dissolve the sugar in a small bit of hot water first. Measurements are not hard and fast and depend upon personal taste. Raspberry or blackberry wine can be made by following any standard wine recipe. Perhaps the most noted use of either raspberries or blackberries is as a fresh fruit. A bowl of fresh berries with real cream and a sprinkling of sugar is a summertime delight that must not be missed. Recipes for raspberry and blackberry jams and jellies are found on the insert that comes with every package of commercially produced pectin. Since the berries lack natural pectin, the store-bought variety is needed to make the jelly set.

Wild raspberries have round stems, covered with prickly spines. The leaves come in groups of three on adult canes and are compound, with from five to seven leaflets on younger canes. The leaves are wrinkled, roughly toothed, and light colored underneath. Blackberries have long, arched, angled stems, with curved spines. The leaves are double toothed and are whitish beneath.

Often, raspberries and blackberries grow in such dense colonies that it is impossible to walk through them. It helps to wear a long-sleeved shirt when picking either berry, as well as stout trousers—either canvas or new unwashed blue jeans. Don't buy the prewashed blue jeans; instead, select the old-fashioned, stiff variety. Berry picking is tedious, but relaxing work. And the end result more than justifies the effort.

Wild Strawberry
Fragaria virginiana

Use: Trail nibble, jam, jelly, dessert

Range: Throughout New England

Similarity to toxic species: None

Best time: June

Status: Common and abundant

Tools needed: None

> Blessings on thee, little man,
> Barefoot boy with cheek of tan!
> With thy turned-up pantaloons,
> And thy merry whistled tunes;
> With thy red lip, redder still
> Kissed by strawberries on the hill . . .
> *John Greenleaf Whittier*

For me, nothing triggers memories of childhood like the fragrance of wild strawberries. Picking these remarkably sweet little berries was one of my favorite youthful pastimes. Once, only a few years ago, my car broke down and I had to walk home along an unpaved country road. Suddenly, I recalled sensations from my boyhood. Then a familiar scent stopped me in my tracks. Wild strawberries. A closer look revealed an extensive patch of dead-ripe wild strawberries a few feet off the road. My car troubles were forgotten for the next hour as my mind and energies centered upon picking and eating as many of these deliciously sweet fruits as was possible.

Wild strawberries are much smaller than the cultivated kind. Even so, the tame berries don't hold a candle to their diminutive wild cousins when it comes to sweetness.

As an adult, with adult duties and responsibilities, I sometimes feel guilty about taking time to pick a half pint box of wild strawberries. But instead of allowing such society-bred guilt to rule, I wade into the task with renewed vigor, determined to pick not just a half pint but a whole pint. To forsake such simple pleasures as picking wild strawberries would be not only wrong, but practically indecent!

Wild strawberries grow primarily on poor soil, in full sun and semishade. The leaflets have coarse teeth, have prominent veins, and grow in groups of three. Wild strawberries and their leaves are a rich source of vitamin C. A strong tea, made by steeping the leaves in boiling water, is a pleasant, vitamin-filled beverage. As with the fruit of brambles, be sure to use strawberry leaves either fresh or perfectly dry. The wilted leaf can be toxic.

My favorite method of preserving wild strawberries is to sprinkle a containerful with sugar and stir the berries until they are fully coated. Then I let them sit on the shelf at room temperature until the sugar combines with the berries to make a syrup. This takes only about ten minutes. The berries are immediately frozen. A dish of wild strawberries is a remarkable cabin-fever reliever during the dark and dreary days of a long New England winter.

Wild strawberry roots were traditionally used as ersatz toothbrushes by various Indian peoples. The ripe berries, too, are said to aid in dental hygiene when crushed and rubbed on the teeth and gums. Whether this works or not, it is certainly a pleasant way to begin one of our brief, glorious days in June.

Highbush Cranberry
Viburnum trilobum

Color plate: Figure 76

Use: Sauce, jelly

Range: Throughout New England

Similarity to toxic species: None, but the non-native Guelder Rose *(V. opulus)* looks much like the Highbush Cranberry. Guelder Rose fruit is strong and bitter, but not toxic.

Best time: October through early spring

Status: Common and abundant

Tools needed: None

One way to truly appreciate the bounty of nature is to take a sunny October afternoon and drive around the New England countryside, picking the fruit of the Highbush Cranberry. It's a member of the honeysuckle family, unrelated to true cranberries. The fruits are often available in startling quantities. A single mile of road in Highbush Cranberry country could yield thousands of pounds of berries. These berries, if not picked by man or bird, persist throughout the winter and, because freezing improves their flavor, can be harvested throughout the season, or until the return of warm weather spoils them.

Highbush Cranberries grow on tall shrubs, rather than vines, as might be expected of something called "cranberry." The coarsely toothed leaves look rather like those of a red maple, with three pointed lobes. The white, rounded flower clusters have smaller flowers in the center, larger ones on the margins. When partially ripe, the berries exhibit a striking combination of red and bright yellow. They become completely red when mature. Highbush Cranberries are shrubs of the roadsides and hedgerows but sometimes grow along streams and brooks.

To make a cranberry sauce substitute out of Highbush Cranberries, fill a large saucepan (an enameled seafood steamer works well) with berries and add water just until the top layer of berries floats. Next, add the rind of one orange. This is needed to render the smelly oils found in the Highbush Cranberries more tolerable. Simmer for about five minutes and mash the berries through a coarse sieve or colander to remove the seeds. Add sugar to taste, along with a package of pectin to make the sauce jell. Additionally, the juice can be used alone, as a concentrated form of Highbush Cranberry juice. Be sure to dilute it with water and to add sugar to taste.

For me, Highbush Cranberries represent the best that a New England autumn has to offer.

Sweetfern
Comptonia peregrina

Color plate: Figure 77

Use: Tea, stimulant (lively aroma lifts the spirits)

Range: Throughout New England

Similarity to toxic species: None

Best time: June through September

Status: Common and abundant

Tools needed: None

Sweetfern, far from being a fern, is a small shrub in the wax myrtle family. It has woody branches that, in late spring, sprout fragrant leaves. And though the branches, too, are fragrant and can be picked and sniffed in winter, it is the leaves that are used to make a refreshing tea.

Over the years, on my various travels around New England, the common Sweetfern is like a letter from home; no matter the location, from northern Maine to the White Mountains of New Hampshire and the bustling cities of southern New England, the plant is always present. Whether on a rural hillside or an unused city lot, Sweetfern can be counted upon, which is more than can be said for many things.

My favorite use of Sweetfern is to pick the leaves, crush them, and stuff them into my shirt pocket. Then, while I walk, the zesty aroma wafts over me, lifting my spirits, reminding me how great it is to be alive. If this were all Sweetfern had to offer, it would be quite enough. But there is more.

A fragrant tea is made from an infusion of the leaves. This is mostly drunk for pleasure and relaxation, though it was once used medicinally because of its astringent qualities. Sweetfern tea has fallen into disuse for medicinal purposes, but its almost cloying fragrance ranks it as a favorite and beloved tea plant.

Older Sweetfern bushes can approach 5 feet in height and twice that in diameter. The slender, segmented leaves resemble fern pinna (the smaller, individual leaflets of a true fern), hence the name *Sweetfern*. Also notice that *Sweetfern* is one word instead of two, which helps make the distinction between it and any particular type of true fern—Sensitive Fern, Ostrich Fern, and so on.

Whether or not Sweetfern was ever used as an oracle is a matter of conjecture. But in the song of the same name, by the famous country group the Carter Family, a girl asks the Sweetfern if her darling is still true. Perhaps this cosmopolitan shrub has more going for it than we know. It's fun to imagine, anyway.

Dandelion
Taraxacum officinale

Color plate: Figure 78

Synonyms: Spring greens, Piss-in-the-Bed

Use: Cooked vegetable, salad, wine ingredient, beverage, medicinal tonic

Range: Throughout New England

Similarity to toxic species: None

Best time: April, May, and October

Status: Abundant and despised as an aggressive weed

Tools needed: An old hunting knife or even a screwdriver may be used to uproot dandelions. Commercially made dandelion diggers are cheaply bought. These, ironically, are made specifically to rid lawns of dandelions. It is fitting, then, for the forager to use them to harvest dandelions for the table.

When New England people say they are going after some greens, they mean dandelions. This European immigrant—brought here purposely, by the way—is firmly entrenched in the culture of the region, both in folklore and in the cuisine of the common people. And now the lowly dandelion has acquired a distinct air of respectability: It is sold in health food stores and even supermarkets throughout New England.

In my youth a common question in springtime among Maine people was, "Did you have your dandelions yet?" The question presupposed that the person cared enough about dandelions to go out and dig some. This, too, speaks volumes about how much New Englanders like their dandelions.

In days past it was known that dandelions contained valuable medicinal properties. The scientific name, *Taraxacum officinale,* indicates that the dandelion was once an official plant medicine of the apothecaries, the forerunners of today's druggists. A high vitamin A and C content, plus the presence of vitamins B and D, potassium, iron, and other minerals, explains the dandelion's effectiveness. Country people to this day consider the first meal of dandelion leaves, crowns, and buds to be a "tonic," just what the doctor ordered to stimulate a sluggish digestion, improve liver function, and generally tone the body and bring it up to snuff. And guess what? The plain old dandelion truly is something of a panacea to the winter-weary body and soul. Folk wisdom, after all, usually has some degree of merit.

As early in the spring as the dandelions are big enough to spot, they are big enough to pick. Granted, the bigger, fuller dandelions of mid-May provide considerably more substance, but the frail, tender dandelions of early spring are the mildest and, no doubt, most appreciated of all. I like to look on the south side of my house, and on sunny, southern slopes. That's where the first little dandelions of the year are going to be found. Dandelion leaves and crowns are wonderful salad ingredients, but my first choice to use them is as boiling greens. Nothing assures me that all is right with the world, that spring has officially arrived, as much as that first steaming-hot mess of cooked dandelion leaves and crowns.

Dig the dandelions roots and all, if possible. Take care to dislodge as much dirt, sand, earthworms, and grit as possible in the field. This will make the final cleaning much easier. I like to clean and rinse my dandelions and then soak them in a pan of lightly salted water for an hour before using them. Then, separate the different parts of the plant. The roots can be peeled, chopped, and boiled for fifteen minutes. The leaves are steamed or boiled for at least ten minutes, and the crowns, along with any unopened buds, are boiled for fifteen minutes, drained, and served with salt, pepper, butter, and sometimes apple cider vinegar.

Dandelions freeze well, and are superb subjects for the home canner. In years past dandelions were preserved in yet another way. I learned of this around 1972, when a friend visited and presented me a gift, a quart of what he called "slack-salted dandelion greens." As he explained it to me, the dandelions were put up in an earthenware crock, a layer of dandelions and a layer of pickling salt, alternating the plants and the salt until the crock was full. My friend had, interestingly, bought this somewhat archaic product from an old-time grocery store in Belfast, Maine. The store has since gone out of business. Other goodies commonly sold there were codfish tongues and cheeks, pickled whelks (locally known as "sea conks"), homemade mustard pickles, old-fashioned store cheese, and smoked alewives, called "bloaters" by Maine people. How I miss that store!

In late spring and through the summer, dandelions are too bitter to eat. Basically, as soon as the plants flower, the season is over. But after the first few frosts, the bitter element is mostly dispelled and dandelions are again superb table fare.

Dandelion roots are a coffee substitute. They must be peeled and slowly roasted in an oven until crisp, then ground before using. This can take up to four hours—too long for me to bother with, no matter how good the ersatz coffee beverage tastes. I would rather eat the dandelions and drink any of the practically numberless wild teas.

Dandelions probably don't need describing, but nonetheless, here it goes. The leaves are deeply lobed, and the hollow stem exudes a milky latex when broken. This latex is one of the bitterest substances imaginable. The golden-yellow blossoms shine in the sun, and each tiny seed is carried about on the wind by a white, fluffy "parachute."

Dandelion blossoms can be made into a sweet, potent wine. This strong wine is practically narcotic in action and should be taken only in small doses.

The finest dandelions will be found on the edges of lawns and driveways, places where they are not subject to attack from the lawn mower. Finally, it goes without saying that dandelions, or any other wild food plant, should never be harvested from any lawn where weed killer has been applied.

Ground Ivy
Glechoma hederacea

Color plate: Figure 79

Synonyms: Gill-Over-the-Ground, Alehoof

Use: Tea, bitter tonic

Range: Throughout New England

Similarity to toxic species: None

Best time: April through November

Status: Common weed of lawns and waste places

Tools needed: None

Ground Ivy is an attractive ground cover, and it's a mystery to me why homeowners don't appreciate this low-growing plant, with its hoof-shaped, ruffled leaves and attractive, wee flowers. But Ground Ivy, despite its good looks and several uses, is almost universally reviled as an invasive, no-good "weed."

A friend has a little wood yard behind his barn, a place where he saws his annual supply of firewood into stove-length sections. Sawdust, wood chips, old asphalt shingles, and rotting pine boards make this a no-man's-land for most plants. That the determined Ground Ivy thrives here is indicative of its tenacity.

Ground Ivy is the source of a pleasant, healthful tea as well as an appetite-stimulating tonic. To use as a tea, chop a small handful (the amount of plant material can vary, according to taste) of fresh Ground Ivy leaves, place them in a teacup, and pour in boiling water. Let the tea steep for a few minutes. It helps to place a saucer over the teacup in order to retain both the heat and the volatile oils of the Ground Ivy.

For use as a bitter tonic (my favorite use, by the way), simply refrigerate the tea and sip a few ounces, cold, about twenty minutes before a meal. This tonic helps stimulate the appetite—and in my experience it makes food taste better. Taking bitters before meals was once as common a practice as having a cup of coffee first thing in the morning is today. Sadly, bitters imbibers are far and few between nowadays. This paucity of adherents is the reason those wonderful, old-time bitters companies are all out of business. To my knowledge, only one company currently manufactures bitters, and while these are of good quality, they are much too expensive for my wee purse. Except for the occasional splurge, I find it cheaper to make my own bitters. And Ground Ivy is the main ingredient.

Ground Ivy is rich in vitamin C, which helps explain why it is so useful when given hot to someone with a cold. Plants such as Ground Ivy and other wild sources of the C vitamin could, if used by more people, replace the vitamin pill. While that is not likely to happen, it is comforting to know that the weeds that grow unbidden all around us are there to help us whenever we wish to turn to them.

Ground Ivy has square stems, which help identify it as one of the mints. It is interesting to note that a plant can be a mint yet lack the characteristic "minty" aroma. Ground Ivy seldom grows more than 5 or 6 inches tall. The tiny violet-blue flowers grow from the leaf axils. The rounded leaves are roughly toothed.

New England Aster
Aster novae-angliae

Color plate: Figure 80

Synonyms: Aster

Use: Cut flowers

Range: Throughout New England

Similarity to toxic species: None

Best time: Late August through October

Status: Common weed

Tools needed: Knife

Why include something that cannot be eaten in a book about foraging? Because beauty, as exhibited in the showy New England Aster, is food for the spirit. What could complement a meal of freshly harvested wild foods better than a fresh-picked bouquet of brilliantly colored wildflowers?

The New England Aster is an icon for the glory days of late summer and early fall. Here in New England, the September air is clean and crisp. Cerulean skies and powder-puff white clouds call for extended walks afield. And to remind us that there is more to life than food, the New England Aster brightens our days for a brief, glorious season.

In shades of violet, magenta, pink, and sometimes rose, the New England Aster is a pioneer plant. Even the roughest of roadside embankments are quickly colonized by this magnificent wildflower. Disturbed ground and waste places don't stay barren long, not if New England Asters are nearby. The windborne seeds, carried on tiny white parachutes, find their way to far-off ground to become the crowning beauty of the following season.

Mostly New England Asters grow to about 3 feet tall, but individual plants can reach more than twice that. The stem is hairy but not prickly. The toothless leaves clasp the stem. The daisy-shaped flowers grow in bunches atop the stems.

When cut, the asters last for three or four days in a water-filled vase. During the blooming season, not a day passes that my kitchen table is not graced with a colorful bouquet of asters. When the flowers fade, they are immediately replaced from among the wild asters blooming outside my cottage.

Once, the nearest asters were miles down the road. A few handfuls of the fluffy seeds, strewn about and carried by the wind, changed that in a hurry. Anybody can do the same. Fill a plastic sandwich bag with the seeds and spread them on any waste ground. In time, a rough-looking space becomes a beautiful wildflower garden.

By October's end the vegetable and flower gardens have succumbed to killing frosts. Foraging, except for animal species, is practically done for the season. And to properly complete the annual cycle, a few New England Asters tenaciously cling to life for just a few more days.

10

Animals

New England seashores, lakes, streams, ponds, and wetlands host multiple species of easily harvested common animals. Many of these, while mostly ignored by anglers and hunters, make superb table fare, and as such are perfect quarry for the recreational forager.

Before harvesting any animal, always consult your state or local regulations.

Crayfish
Decapoda astacus

Color plate: Figure 81

Synonyms: Crawfish, crawdad

Use: The cooked tails are eaten and are similar to lobster in flavor and texture. Also used as fish bait.

Range: Throughout New England

Similarity to toxic species: None, but the pincers can inflict a painful wound.

Best time: May and June in brooks and streams, May through September in lakes and ponds

Status: Common and abundant

Tools needed: A collecting pail and rubber boots for handpicking. More sophisticated tools include a wire-mesh minnow trap for overnight use in ponds and lakes. A dip net and a bit of fish or chicken tied to string can be useful for collecting during the day.

On Maine's Moosehead Lake, crayfish grow unusually large. Locals know them by the sobriquet *Moosehead lobster.* It isn't unusual to see strings dangling into the water from private docks. These usually have a bit of fish, or perhaps a chicken wing, tied on the end. The camp owner tends these strings regularly, slowly pulling the bait toward the surface. The crayfish clinging to the bait are reluctant to release their grip and can be scooped in with a long-handled dip net. When enough crayfish are captured, they are steamed until they turn red (crayfish, like lobsters and crabs, are not naturally red, but turn crimson when cooked). Then the tail, the only part worth bothering with, is pulled from the body and its meat is dug out, dipped in melted butter, and consumed with great relish.

My first dish of crayfish was obtained in an amusing way. While I was fishing a local lake, a good-sized smallmouth bass hit my lure. When the fish was netted, a 3-inch-long crayfish popped out of its mouth. The crayfish was still alive; it had evidently only just then been caught by the bass, which in turn was only just then caught by me. Bass and crayfish both went into my cooler, and as a side dish with my bass fillets that evening I tried my first steamed crayfish. It was, of course, delicious, and indeed comparable to lobster. Foraging for crayfish immediately became a serious pastime.

The simplest way to catch crayfish is to visit a stream or brook, turn over underwater rocks, and wait for the current to wash away any mud or silt. If a crayfish is present, it will be immediately visible when the water clears, its pincher claws held aloft in a gesture of defiance. The crayfish can be then scooped up in a simple, homemade net, or taken by hand. The manual method is a challenge. While keeping the animal's attention with one hand (making sure the little critter doesn't grab hold of a finger), slowly move your other hand behind the crayfish—they move backward when frightened—and grasp the body. Plunk the crayfish in a pail and look for another one.

A wire minnow trap is probably a more effective way to capture crayfish. These are cheaply bought, or can be made of $1/4$-inch hardware cloth. The dimensions for this trap are unimportant—they truly depend upon how much hardware cloth you have on hand. However, for those who like more exacting directions, the trap can be from 1 to 3 feet long and from 8 to 20 inches round. The wire mesh is rolled into any length to form a tube. Then two other pieces of mesh are each formed into a funnel shape, the mouths of the funnels measuring the same diameter as the tube. Insert the funnels, narrow-end first, into either end of the tube, and use the loose ends of wire to attach the funnels to the tube openings. Then, with wire cutters, cut a square from the side of the tube and refasten it loosely. This is removed to empty the trap once the crayfish enter it.

Bait the trap with any meat, poultry, or fish. Tie the trap to a stout cord and place it underwater in a shallow section of a pond or lake. It's best to leave the trap overnight and check it the next morning. With luck, it will be filled with lively crayfish.

Most people who own small ponds that have become infested with crayfish are only too happy to allow a forager to trap the critters. That's because the crayfish muddy the water by building nests in the banks. Such private ponds can provide a practically endless source of crayfish for the astute forager.

Crayfish are usually dark green in color, although the body can exhibit traces of brown and even tinges of yellow. A detailed description of the physical appearance is unnecessary, because a crayfish resembles a lobster in nearly every way, except for size. Crayfish, except for the unusually large Moosehead Lake variety, average about 3 inches long. Anyone who has seen a lobster knows what a crayfish looks like.

Cooking crayfish "New England style" is a breeze. While the famed Louisiana "crawfish boil" requires added spices and considerable fussing, our eastern method needs only a saucepan and about 2 inches of boiling water. Drop the live crayfish in and cover. Let them cook for perhaps ten minutes, turn off the heat, and dip out the crayfish. This method steams rather than boils the crayfish. Boiling is an acceptable method, of course, but it takes longer to heat the water and, at least to my taste, it seems to render the crayfish rather bland. Steaming seals in the flavor.

Let the cooked crayfish cool for a few moments and, while holding the body with one hand, pull the tail away with the other. The small, dark vein on the outside of the tail meat can be discarded and the end of the tail pinched, in order to make the meat pop out. It may be necessary to partially split the shell of the tail in order to remove the meat, using either fingers or a pocketknife (or, a fancy steak knife, for the more refined forager). Then dip the hot tail meat in melted butter and enjoy.

A mess of steamed crayfish can be the crowning touch to any camping trip. Just don't forget the butter.

Bullfrog
Rana catesbeiana

Color plate: Figure 82

Use: The skinned, fried legs are a delicacy.

Range: Throughout New England, but scarce in far northern Maine. Because of the popularity of frog's legs as table fare, bullfrogs have been successfully introduced into the American West, dramatically increasing their range.

Similarity to toxic species: None

Best time: Summer and early fall

Status: Bullfrogs are common and abundant throughout their range.

Tools needed: You can catch bullfrogs by hand or with a homemade frog spear. A slingshot or a bit of red cloth on a fishhook will also work. Kill bullfrogs by hitting them on the head with a heavy stick or a short bit of metal water pipe.

Once, after I had spoken to a group about frogs, a woman asked me what a female frog is called. This puzzled me, and she explained that since a male frog was called a bullfrog, it seemed likely that a female frog should have a separate title as well. She was surprised to learn that the term *bullfrog* refers to a specific kind of frog, and not to any distinction between the sexes.

It often amazes people to find that bullfrogs are not the meek, mild creatures they are commonly thought to be. Instead of patiently sitting on lily pads waiting for bugs to pass within grabbing range, bullfrogs are aggressive predators, and sometimes even cannibalistic. They are known to eat small mammals, frogs, salamanders, newts, snakes, small turtles, baby birds, spiders, snails, insects, and crayfish.

One summer a horde of bullfrogs arrived at my farm pond. The frogs mostly stayed on a small island in the middle of the pond, pretty much out of sight and out of mind (except for the occasional deep, thundering *jug-o'-rum* call). One day I decided to throw some stale bread to the minnows in the pond. The little fish soon located the treat, and dozens of them swirled on top, feeding heartily. Then a bullfrog jumped into the water and, swimming ever so slowly, positioned itself in the center of the feeding minnows. Suddenly the frog lunged for and captured a minnow. Then a larger frog, watching from the island, jumped in and quickly approached the first frog. The smaller frog tried to hold its ground but was forced to retreat after the larger animal bit it savagely and repeatedly. The victor claimed rights to capture the minnows and protected its turf by attacking and driving off any frog that came within range. This behavior completely changed my way of thinking about bullfrogs. It's a good thing that bullfrogs don't get as large as house cats; they would be a danger to people!

There was scarcely a country boy in days past who had not killed a few bullfrogs and cooked himself a mess of frog legs. In my time, frog hunting was a rite of passage. Perhaps our youthful culinary endeavors were a bit crude, but truthfully, fancy frog leg cookery differs little from the primitive method employed by youngsters. Just roll the legs in flour or cornmeal and pan-fry to a golden brown. Salt and pepper complement fried frog legs.

To prepare the legs, make a slit around where the thickest part of the leg joins the body. Leaving the legs attached to the frog, grab the skin with pliers and pull toward the feet. With the skin hanging around the feet, cut off the feet and discard skin and feet. Then, with a sharp knife, disjoint the skinned legs where they join the body. Discard the body—there's no meat on it worth bothering about.

Once, at a party, the host offered frog legs packed in cans, like sardines or smoked oysters. They were pretty good, but they didn't hold a candle to the fresh, fried variety.

The discriminating connoisseur of fine foods pays fancy prices for frog legs in posh restaurants. Self-reliant foragers catch and prepare their own frog legs and don't pay a cent.

Frogs and amphibians in general may be in trouble. Declining numbers and physical abnormalities have become a concern to scientists. While theories abound as to the cause, no single factor has been identified. Airborne chemicals, ultraviolet rays, viruses, and a host of other factors are all suspected. A clear answer, however, is yet to be found; the question is still wholly up in the air.

Foragers who stick to hunting bullfrogs, which are common and abundant, need not worry about unduly affecting local populations. Also, fish and game departments generally don't regulate frog hunting. However, some special measures have been taken to prevent predicted frog extinctions. In one western state concerned folks have petitioned the fish and wildlife department to end its trout-stocking program in a large watershed on the grounds that trout eat the tadpoles, endangering the frogs. This, in my fifty-odd years of trout fishing, is something I have never seen. In examining many hundreds of trout stomachs, never has a tadpole been present. And in observing trout behavior, never have I seen a trout exhibit the slightest interest in a tadpole. Conversely, bullfrogs can and do eat young trout. I give this as an example of how well-intended people sometimes act without sufficient reason or cause. Then again, perhaps western trout differ in their tastes from our eastern trout.

Because some frogs (and other amphibians) are becoming scarce, or even disappearing, it is worthwhile for us to study the situation. Toward that end, there are various ways in which average citizens may contribute to the body of knowledge. One way is to participate in Frogwatch USA, a program that monitors frog activity by assessing data collected by volunteers. The program, which can be joined over the Internet or by phone or mail, assigns observer numbers to volunteers, who, during the breeding season, regularly visit vernal pools and wetlands to record what kind of frog calls are heard, and the intensity of the calls.

Participation in Frogwatch USA is a wonderful way to involve children in nature. It's real, firsthand experience and, as such, beats reading about the thing in a book. Adults, me included, benefit too, if only because the monitoring sessions are so enjoyable. To learn more about Frogwatch USA, go online and contact www.mp2-pwrc.usgs.gov/frogwatch. Or write to: Frogwatch Coordinator, USGS PWRC, 12100 Beech Forest Road, Laurel, MD 20708-4038, phone (301) 497–5819.

Freshwater Mussels

Color plate: Figure 83

Synonyms: Freshwater clams

Use: Edible as emergency survival food

Range: Mussels are found throughout New England, but all mussels do not exist in all states. Some are widely dispersed. For instance, the federally endangered dwarf wedgemussel, *Alasmidonta heterodon,* is believed to have been extirpated from its native range of all the New England states and is now only found in the Connecticut River watershed. At the same time, the eastern lampmussel, *Lampsilis radiata radiata,* is found in all six New England states and in much of Canada.

Similarity to toxic species: None

Best time: Anytime, as long as waters are free of ice

Status: Freshwater mussel populations vary widely from state to state. Maine has the largest number of suitable waters in New England. Some mussels hold their own in some New England states and are either not present or considered to be species of special concern in others. For the most up-to-date information on this fascinating subject, order a copy of *The Freshwater Mussels of Maine* by Ethan Nedear, Mark A. McCollough, and Beth I. Swartz, Maine Department of Inland Fisheries and Wildlife, State House Station #41, Augusta, ME 04333-0041. Send a check for $10.00 plus $2.00 shipping, payable to Endangered and Nongame Wildlife Fund. This book is an amazing source of information on mussel biology, the distribution of freshwater mussels in Maine and New England, details of each species, and their current status.

Tools needed: None

If you've ever held a freshwater mussel, you've probably wondered if it was good to eat. The answer is yes and no. Freshwater mussels are edible, but they're not tasty. I know—I've tried. And as long-lived filter feeders, mussels can concentrate in their flesh some of the meaner toxins found in our environment. More important, many mussels are in danger, or are on the brink of being endangered or threatened. But because it would be possible for a lost, starving person to gain sustenance from freshwater mussels, I've included them here. In anything but an emergency situation, however, mussels should be admired and not disturbed.

Freshwater mussels are creatures of shallow sections of ponds and lakes, as well as fast- and slow-moving streams. It often amazes people when, for the first time, they become aware of large colonies of shellfish living in fresh water. Look for mussels in shallow water where they can be plainly seen, partially imbedded in the mud. They are of various shapes and usually are about the size of a child's hand. Mussels travel only a short distance in their long lifetime but can move to deeper water if water levels drop. The presence of mussels can often be determined at a glance by the sometimes large piles of shells found on the shore, evidence of a muskrat feast. These aquatic mammals are fond of mussels and don't discriminate between the stable and the endangered varieties.

Mussels are the "canaries" of many of our inland waters. The plight of mussels can be attributed to many factors, including pollution, dams, and even acid rain. When a species of mussels is gone, what or who may be next?

Mussels contribute much to the ecology of our lakes, ponds, and streams. They are filter feeders, taking in large amounts of water—from $1/2$ to $1\frac{1}{4}$ gallons per hour—and filtering out small particles of food. They serve both to clean the water and return valuable nutrients for different plant species to thrive upon.

Common Blue Mussel
Mytilus edulis

Color plate: Figure 84

Synonyms: Blue mussel, mussel

Use: Cooked seafood, pickled snack

Range: Along the entire New England seashore

Similarity to toxic species: None

Best time: Blue mussels are available year-round.

Status: Common and abundant

Tools needed: None

The scientific name for the common blue mussel of the New England seashore reveals its most valuable feature: *Mytilus edulis* means "edible mussel." Mussels were once scorned by New Englanders, taking a backseat to the more widely accepted clams and oysters. Today, no longer relegated to obscurity, the common blue mussel has gained regional acceptance and is a common item on restaurant menus and in the seafood cooler at grocery stores. Mussel farming, the practice of producing large, grit-free mussels, is a thriving new industry in New England.

But it is the wild variety of the blue mussel that concerns foragers. After periwinkles, mussels are our most abundant shellfish. As compared to digging clams, which is hard labor at best, picking mussels is like a walk in the park. Vast colonies of mussels lie exposed each time the tide goes out. It is possible to gather enough for a meal in a matter of minutes. The mussels produce a "holdfast" or "beard"—a tangled mass of threadlike filaments used by mussels to anchor themselves to rocks or even to other mussels. The beard, properly termed a byssus, may be removed when the mussel is picked, or left on and used to grasp the meat after the mussel is cooked.

Mussel shells range in color from black to navy blue. Each half of the 2- to 3-inch shell is deeply concave. The body of the mussel is generally orange. These sometimes turn creamy white when cooked.

Any kind of container may be used when picking mussels, but most serious mussel harvesters prefer wood or wire-mesh clam baskets, or rollers. These can be sloshed in the water to remove any clinging mud or grit from the mussels. For a cheap and easy substitute, a common nylon mesh bag fills the role wonderfully. These can be purchased, or, for the thrifty forager, a second hand onion bag works just fine. Anything that allows the water to drain is acceptable. Never carry or store mussels submerged in water.

My preferred method is to place the mussels in a cooler upon returning to my vehicle from the mussel beds. Upon reaching home, the mussels are again rinsed and then placed in the refrigerator, where they can be safely stored for several days. They never last that long at my house.

Mussels lend themselves to countless recipes. The following are only a select few of my favorites. Remember that mussels are an important part of French cuisine; that country has devised innumerable elegant ways to prepare them. Do delve into the many and fascinating ways to use these free gifts of the sea; the experiment can last a lifetime.

Steamed mussels are not the plebeian fare many might suppose. The key to a memorable meal of steamed mussels is to steam the bivalves in their own juices. It is likely that one of the reasons mussels have taken so long to gain appreciation from the general public is that most people know only boiled, rather than steamed, mussels. To place fresh mussels in a great pot of boiling water is a sin. The resulting product tastes like cardboard, with nothing to recommend it except that it contains many vitamins and trace minerals. My grandmother cooked clams and mussels this way. It was the old school of seafood cookery, and that's where it deserves to stay, old and far away, preferably forgotten.

Instead, place the mussels in a pot, cover, and turn the heat to high. It's that simple. The natural juices contained within the mussel are released within minutes. When the pot bubbles and froth creeps over the edge, set the cover so that the steam can escape and turn down the heat to medium. Cook until all the mussel shells gape open. To serve, lift the shells out of the pan with a slotted spoon or similar utensil and then drain and reserve the broth, or "nectar," in a small bowl to be used as a final rinse for the mussel meats. Although some like to add melted butter to the nectar, it is superfluous and, I believe, harms the delicate flavor. At the end of the meal, the nectar can be drunk. This rich broth is the crowning touch to a simple but hearty and flavorful meal.

The basic steamed mussel recipe can be tweaked, though. The addition of a slight amount of crushed garlic, an ounce of sherry, and some thin-sliced onion, placed in the pot with the fresh mussels, imparts a delicate texture to the basic mussel flavor. This is my favorite mussel recipe and to me represents the pinnacle of mussel cookery. Amounts of each ingredient must be determined according to each individual's taste.

Here is a recipe that utilizes leftover mussel meats. This is a favorite of old-time Downeast residents. Here again, amounts of each ingredient are determined according to taste and according to the size of the vessel used. Begin by picking out the cooked mussel meats from the shells and placing them on a plate. Next, slice an onion as thinly as possible. Line the bottom of a clean, screw-top jar with the mussels and then top with a layer of onion slices. Keep alternating mussel meats and onion slices until the jar is nearly full. Then tuck several Northern Bay leaves (don't substitute commercial bay leaves) on the inside of the jar, between the glass and the mussels. Fill the jar to the top with white vinegar and tap to release any trapped air. Add more vinegar if needed. Allow to stand in the refrigerator for at least three or four days. The mussels will keep in the refrigerator for several weeks.

Mussels in pesto are a summertime delight. Steam the mussels and remove the meats. Slather them with room-temperature, homemade pesto. This simple meal can be eaten as is, or used to top pasta.

The possibilities being endless, my last suggestion is to experiment, experiment. There is no wrong way to cook blue mussels!

Periwinkle
Littorina littorea

Color plate: Figure 85

Synonyms: Common periwinkle, wink

Use: Cooked shellfish

Range: Throughout New England

Similarity to toxic species: None

Best time: Year-round

Status: Common and plentiful

Tools needed: None

Common periwinkles are said to grow to 1 inch in diameter, but they're almost always a bit smaller than that. The spiral shells come in various shades of brown and are sometimes tinged with yellow. Rocks near the high-tide line are covered with these plentiful mollusks. Although periwinkles appear to be stationary, they are constantly on the move, albeit at a snail's pace.

Although easy to harvest and delicious when boiled, few people bother with periwinkles, probably because, like dandelions, they are too common. Or perhaps nobody knows that periwinkles are eminently edible. For whatever reason, it is their loss. For the astute forager, periwinkles are, mostly because of their commonness and great abundance, a high-priority item.

It is easy to pick periwinkles. Grasp them, pull them from the rock, and drop them in a container. It takes lots to make a meal, so collect at least a pint per person.

Back at home, put the periwinkles in water to make sure they are all alive. Dead ones will float, live ones sink. Rinse well and drain. Next, boil water in a medium-sized saucepan. A few tablespoons of salt added to the water will make the periwinkle meats a bit resilient—all the better for removing them from the spiraled shell. Boil for about five minutes. Be careful not to overcook, which will make the meat tough. By the way, this boiling, rather than steaming, is necessary because boiling introduces the salt to the periwinkle, where as steaming would not. Remove the periwinkles from the water, drain, and place on a serving dish. The meat can be removed from the shell with a toothpick, a nutpick, or even a common finishing nail.

Nobody ever gained weight by eating too many periwinkles. Like the popular commercial snack, it is impossible to "eat just one," but unlike the store-bought item, some time must elapse between mouthfuls. It takes a moment to stab the periwinkle meat and pull it from the shell. Eating periwinkles is a hands-on activity for the do-it-yourselfer.

If enough periwinkles remain after cooking a batch, they may be treated the same as the common blue mussel and pickled in white vinegar. Consult the chapter on mussels (page 168) for the recipe.

When harvesting periwinkles, be prepared to be the subject of odd looks from passersby. It's amusing to imagine what the people think when they see a periwinkle harvester. "I wonder what that nut is going to do with all those little snails?" Or perhaps they take pity, seeing some poor soul reduced to eating periwinkles. Little do they know that instead of being the poor tatterdemalion, the forager is taking advantage of one of New England's tastiest seafoods.

Atlantic Razor Clam
Ensis directus

Color plate: Figure 86

Synonyms: Razor clam

Use: Razor clam meats are used fresh or cooked in a variety of recipes.

Range: Found throughout coastal New England

Similarity to toxic species: None

Best time: Year-round

Status: Locally abundant

Tools needed: Razor clams can be harvested by hand, but a handheld trowel, a garden spade, or a standard clam hoe will make the process easier.

Once, many years ago, a section of clam flats near my Belfast, Maine, home was opened to harvesting for the first time in twenty-five years. Locals, knowing it held huge surf clams, flocked to the place. Besides surf clams we found vast numbers of razor clams. It was there that a scene unfolded that is deeply etched in my memory. A big man with a long red beard sat on a rock and with a jackknife deftly opened one Razor Clam after another and ate them raw, biting pieces off as one would a pickle. He continued opening and chewing the clams as he talked with me.

Small razor clams—no longer than a person's index finger—are excellent raw, although unlike old Red Beard, I like to take them home to prepare and serve them, rather than consume them on the beach. It is easy to open razor clams because they cannot close their shells completely. A sharp knife can lay the shell open, where the meat is easily removed. It is nice to place the meat back in the shells and serve them on a platter of crushed ice. Finishing touches include a few sprigs of fresh parsley and some lemon wedges, artistically arranged on the edge of the platter. Squeeze a bit of lemon juice on the raw clam, pick it up with a small seafood fork, and enjoy!

Steamed razor clams are superb, rivaling common steamer clams for taste. As with mussels, don't use any water; the razor clams contain more than enough natural juice for steaming them. And as with mussels, reserve the broth for dipping and later drinking. Steam the clams until the shells are completely open and the clam meat has shrunk to about half its raw size.

Larger razor clams can be chopped and used in fritters, as baked stuffed clams, and clam chowder. See surf clam, pages 177–78, for baking recipes.

Cooking razor clams is easy. Harvesting them can be tricky. Razor clams are so called because they so closely resemble an old-fashioned straight-edged razor. The analogy is made complete by the edges of the shells, which are nearly as sharp as a razor. Be careful when harvesting them.

To find razor clams, walk the clam flats on a low tide—the lower the better. Look for airholes in the sand. Because razor clams can move through the sand at amazingly fast speeds, tread lightly to avoid warning them of your presence. With a clam hoe, a hand trowel, or even a spade, quickly turn over the sand. Even if you don't see a clam, carefully stick a hand in the bottom of the hole. It is possible to grasp the fleeing clam by the end of the shell. Here is where the rash forager can end up with a nasty slice on the fingers, so don't try to pull the clam up immediately. Instead, hold on with a steady pressure. Anyone who has ever picked nightcrawlers will understand the technique. In a few moments the clam will relax its grip and can be easily pulled from the hole.

Lacking tools, razor clams can be taken by inserting your hand in the sand on top of the clam's airhole. But do so cautiously, on account of the sharp edge of the clamshell.

Razor clams are up to 7 inches long when mature. They appear brown, because their shells are covered with a thin, dark outer layer called a periostracum. This coating deteriorates when the clam dies and the shell returns to its true white color. The clam moves by means of a long, muscular appendage called a foot. It can change the shape of the foot at will. To move downward, into the sand, the razor clam lengthens the foot until it is quite slender. The long, thin appendage is then thrust as far as possible in the sand. Then the end of the foot is formed into a knob, which the clam uses as an anchor. All it needs to do now is contract the foot, and the clam can zip through the sand with great speed and ease.

Razor clams are not sold commercially because they don't keep well. To enjoy the tantalizing, rich flavor of these unique shellfish, it is necessary to go out and harvest them yourself. For the forager, that is a blessing, not a problem.

Surf Clam
Spisula solidissima

Color plate: Figure 87

Synonyms: Hen clam, quahog

Use: Chowder or fritter ingredient, as baked, stuffed clams, and in homemade clam sauce for pasta. The adductor muscle can be cooked or eaten raw.

Range: Throughout New England

Similarity to toxic species: None

Best time: Throughout the year at very low tide

Status: Locally common

Tools needed: None is necessary, but a spading fork or clam hoe is a big help.

"Wanna go quahogging?" is what one Maine person might ask another. The questioner here really wants to know if the other person would care to go harvest surf, or hen, clams. Proper designations aside, surf clams are one of our largest clams, sometimes reaching 6 or more inches long and 5 inches wide. Where harvesting is permitted (pollution and toxic shellfish poison, the so-called red tide, sometimes cause closures of the clam flats), the daily possession limit is usually overly liberal. On the other hand, it may as well be, because these giant clams weigh up fast and few people have the physical stamina to carry a full limit from the clam beds back to their vehicle.

Surf clams have thick shells to cope with the pounding the animals receive from waves. When the clams are alive, the shell is coated with a dark film called the periostracum. This is quickly lost when the clam dies. The shells of surf clams litter beaches where the clams live. At one time almost every seaside cottage had a stack of neatly scrubbed surf clam shells that people used as ashtrays. My personal favorite use of the shells, other than in stuffed, baked clams, is to throw them in depressions in my gravel driveway, where they act as long-lasting fill that will not wash away.

Surf clams live in areas that are usually covered with water. A normal low tide does not drain far enough for practical surf clam harvesting. It is only during very low tides that the sandbars and gravel banks so favored by surf clams are exposed. And at that, sometimes a strong onshore wind can back up the tide so that clamming is impeded. Conversely, a run-of-the-mill low tide can be strengthened by an offshore wind to the point that the surf clam beds are exposed. Tide charts, available from most marine supply stores and at sportfishing stores catering to saltwater anglers, are good sources of information on tides throughout the year. Tides in the negative figures are recommended for harvesting surf clams.

It is possible to find the holes made by surf clams by snorkeling the shallow water during a normal low tide. But the best way is to go out during the "spring" or "low-drain" tides and walk the beach near the water's edge at the time of extreme low tide. The surf clams make breathing holes in the sand; these are the giveaway to their presence. To tell the difference between a surf clam hole and those made by inedible sand dollars, place a foot on either side of the hole and bounce up and down. A surf clam will expel water through its siphon, but the sand dollar won't. All that you need do next is carefully work a spading fork (bare hands can do the trick, but the fork makes things easier) under the clam and turn the sand over. With luck, a huge, dark brown surf clam will be exposed, its "foot" or propulsion member wiggling in the air.

Once, while digging surf clams on a local beach, I met a local man who had been there for some time and had a huge basket of clams. While we spoke, a group of obvious tourists approached us and explained that although they had tried for some time, they were unable to locate any of those huge clams. Would we give them any advice? Without a moment's hesitation, the successful clam digger said, "Look for the X." The poor tourists walked away, baffled.

I use a large, wire-mesh egg basket to hold my surf clams. With this, it is easy to swish the clams around in the water and remove most of the clinging sand particles. Anything will do, though. A large onion bag is as good as anything, as is a traditional pack basket.

Back home, with a fresh bunch of surf clams, is where the real work begins. These hard-shell clams are difficult to open, so many folks like to briefly steam them in a little water in order to make the clams open their shells. But this method has its faults. The clam broth is expelled as the clam is heated, and diluted with water. The broth is better when undiluted. And I am convinced that steaming toughens the clam. A better way is to scrub and rinse the clams and place them on the sideboard of the sink. In time, the clams will relax and allow the shell to open, at least enough to get in a knife and, with a twist, open the clam fully.

Try to open each clam over a container, so that the valuable clam juice is reserved separately. Then, with the knife, remove the adductor muscles—those cylinder-shaped muscles that hold the two sections of the shell together. These can be sautéed in butter, with perhaps some fresh herbs added. Serve immediately, while still hot. To me, these treats are tastier than true scallops. Others use the adductor muscles in chowders, but that seems a great waste to me, especially since the rest of the clam is perfectly suited to use in chowder and the tender, sweet adductor muscles are better put to a higher use.

Broiled surf clam adductor muscles are a treat fit for kings and princes. In a glass baking dish, place a pat of butter and arrange the clam muscles. Sprinkle the muscles with fresh (or dried) parsley, freshly ground black pepper, and a bit of paprika. Broil only until the ersatz scallops turn completely white. For a memorable feast, serve with a wild salad and good homemade bread.

The so-called strips, or lengths of flesh along the inside rim of the shell, along with the foot, require additional processing. Use a sharp knife and slice between the strip and the shell to remove the outer strips. The foot must be removed from the body of the clam, rinsed, and set aside with the strips. The only thing remaining is what Mainers call the "stomach." This can be sliced open and rinsed, but that is a lot of trouble and hardly worth the effort. Concentrate on the strips and the feet.

The feet and strips are tough and must be chopped or ground. A hand-powered food grinder set on medium or coarse is perfect. A sharp knife can be used to chop the clam meat, but it is a tedious process. The finished product can be used in several ways.

My favorite method is to grind the clams and, using the cleaned shells, make stuffed, baked clams. Mix the clams with commercially prepared or homemade Italian-style bread crumbs. If the mixture becomes too stiff (because when baked, a stiff mixture will be too dry), add some of the reserved clam juice. Next, chop a green pepper into small pieces and mix with the clams and crumbs. When the mixture is just stiff enough so that it holds itself together, fill a clam shell with it. Continue filling the clam shells until the clam-crumb mixture is used up. The clams can be baked in a 350-degree oven for twenty minutes, or until the outside of the mixture is slightly browned. These stuffed clamshells can be wrapped in aluminum foil and frozen—my personal, wild version of the TV dinner.

The chopped or ground clams can also be put to good use in a pasta sauce. To a half pint of clams, add perhaps three tablespoons of olive oil, some freshly chopped garlic, freshly chopped oregano, and a few sprigs of chopped thyme. A couple turns of the pepper grinder over the mixture will introduce the correct amount of black pepper. I like to let this sauce sit in the refrigerator a day before using it, to allow the flavors to intermingle. Drizzle the heated sauce (don't boil when heating) over your favorite pasta and enjoy!

Clam fritters, using chopped surf clams, are delicious. Use any commerically prepared or homemade pancake batter. Add clams and whatever clam juice accompanies them. I like a thin batter, but for a fluffier fritter, use a higher proportion of clams and liquid to the batter. Fry until slightly browned on both sides.

Chowder is that final use for the chopped surf clam strips and feet. Each person has his or her own favorite chowder recipe, and here is mine. Use a pint of chopped clams. Add from one-half to one pint of the reserved clam juice (this stuff, as well as the chopped clams, can be frozen for later use in chowders and whatnot). To that, add a good handful of chopped onion and one large or two small potatoes, peeled and cubed. Many people add a few small chunks of salt pork to chowders, but I prefer to dispense with that tradition. Do, however, add some freshly ground black pepper.

Next is what separates my chowder from other people's. Simmer the ingredients for about thirty minutes, never allowing the mixture to boil. Add milk only when everything else is cooked. And at that, add only enough so that the chowder is opaque. Milk can drown the flavor of the clams, but when used in limited quantities, it will enhance and contain it. Finally, many will want to add a pat of butter to float on top. Don't. If anybody wants butter, they may add it to their own bowl of chowder. Serve piping hot, with fresh, hot biscuits.

Glossary

Alternate. When leaves are alternately arranged on the stems. This can also be described as leaves that grow singly on the stem.

Basal rosette. When leaves radiate from a central point at the base of the stem. Many plants, when immature and lacking other identifiable features, are easily recognized by the basal rosette.

Bract. A leaflike object that supports a flower cluster, often mistaken for a flower petal. Bunchberry "petals" are actually bracts.

Branchlet. Shoot growth of the current growing season.

Clasping. A leaf that has no stalk and clasps the stem.

Frond. A fern leaf.

Leaf. The stalk and blade of hardwood trees or plants and the needles and scales of conifers. Pine needles, therefore, are really pine leaves.

Margin. The outer edge of a leaf.

Midrib. The large middle vein of a leaf.

Node. Where the leaf attaches to the stem. The part of the stem between the leaves is called the internode.

Opposite. When leaves are arranged opposite one another.

Perfoliate. A leaf that surrounds the stem, making the stem appear to perforate the leaf.

Petal. An inner part of a flower, often colored.

Petiole. The leafstalk.

Rhizome. The underground stem of perennial plants. These often grow horizontally and close to the surface. Rhizomes are not roots, although they are often confused with roots.

Sessile. A leaf without a stalk.

Sheath. A node is sheathed when the leaf wraps around the stem at the node. Lady's Thumb is a fine example of a sheath.

Shoot. New growth. When a plant erupts from the ground in spring, the tender shoots are sometimes harvested.

Simple. A leaf that has a single blade (the flat part of the leaf).

Stipe. The stem of a fern frond.

Stipule. What looks like a tiny, immature leaf at the base of the petiole. These protect the developing young leaf and never grow into leaves themselves.

Teeth. The little "teeth" on the edge of a leaf. These resemble the teeth on a handsaw. Leaves can be finely or coarsely toothed. Some have no teeth and are described as "entire." Certain leaves—some of the oaks, for instance—are not so much toothed as they are lobed.

Umbel. A group of flowers or fruit with stalks attached at a common point. This grouping resembles a reflexed umbrella, hence the word *umbel*.

Veins. Veins are small avenues radiating from the leafstalk, like capillaries in the human body. The sap, with its minerals, water, and various compounds, flows in and out of the veins.

Venation pattern. The way in which the veins are arranged on a leaf. Some are parallel, others pinnate—that is, smaller veins branch from a central, larger main vein.

Wavy. When a leaf margin is smooth but undulating.

Whorl. When two or more leaves originate at the same level on a common axis.

Index

Achillea millefolium, 108–09
Amaranthus retroflexus, 43–44
Amelanchier spp., 64–66
animals, 159
Aralia nudicaulis, 106–07
Arctium lappa, 134–35
Artemisia vulgaris, 122–23
Asclepias syriaca, 132–33
Aster macrophyllus, 54–55
Aster novae-angliae, 157–58
Atlantic razor clam, 173–74
Atriplex patula, 5–6

Beach Peas, 9–10
bees, xv
Black Willow, 98–99
Blackberries, 144–45
bogs, 81
Boneset, 110–11
bullfrog, 163–65
Bunchberry, 56–57

Cakile edentula, 11–12
Caltha palustris, 33–34
Calvatia gigantea (and other Calvatia species), 75–77
Canada Goldenrod, 117–18
Cattail, 82–84

Chenopodium album, 36–38
Chicken of the Woods, 71–72
Clintonia, 50–51
Clintonia borealis, 50–51
common blue mussel, 168–70
Common Blue Violet, 62–63
Common Milkweed, 132–33
Common Plantain, 142–43
Common Saint-John's-Wort, 114–16
Comptonia peregrina, 150–51
Coptis groenlandica, 119–20
Cornus canadensis, 56–57
crayfish, 160–62
Curled Dock, 29–30

Dandelion, 152–54
Decapoda astacus, 160–62
deer ticks, xvii
disturbed and cultivated ground, 35

Eastern Hemlock, 94–95
Ensis directus, 173–74
environmental cautions, xix
Eupatorium maculatum, 121
Eupatorium perfoliatum, 110–11
Evening Primrose, 138–39

fertile streamsides, 21

Field Peppergrass, 41–42
Fragaria virginiana, 146–47
freshwater mussels, 166–67

Galinsoga ciliata (also *G. parviflora* where available), 39–40
Gaultheria procumbens, 58–59
Gem-Studded Puffball, 75–77
giardia, xvi
Glasswort, 13–14
Glechoma hederacea, 155–56
Goldthread, 119–20
Goose Tongue, 2–4
Great Burdock, 134–35
Green Amaranth, 43–44
Grifolia frondosa, 73–74
Ground Ivy, 155–56

harvesting techniques, xv–xvi
Heal-All, 112–13
Hen of the Woods, 73–74
Highbush Cranberry, 148–49
Hypericum perforatum, 114–16

identifying plants, xiv–xv
Impatiens capensis, 129–31
Indian Cucumber, 52–53

Japanese Knotweed, 126–28
Jewelweed, 129–31

Lady's Thumb, 47–48
Laetiporus sulphureus, 71–72
Lamb's-Quarters, 36–38
Large-Leafed Aster, 54–55
Lathyrus japonicus, 9–10
Lepidium campestre, 41–42

Littorina littorea, 171–72
Lycoperdon perlatum, 75–77
Lyme disease, xvii

Marsh Marigold, 33–34
Matricaria matricarioides, 140–41
Medeola virginica, 52–53
medicinal plants, xviii–xix, 101–03
Morchella esculenta, 69–70
Morel, 69–70
Mugwort, 122–23
mushrooms, 67–68
Myrica pensylvanica, 17–18
Mytilus edulis, 168–70

New England, xiii–xiv
New England Aster, 157–58
Northern Bay, 17–18

Oenothera biennis, 138–39
Orache, 5–6
Orpine, 136–37
Ostrich Fern, 22–25
Oyster Mushroom, 78–79

periwinkle, 171–72
Picea rubens, 96–97
Pickerelweed, 85–86
Pineapple Weed, 140–41
Pinus strobus, 92–93
Plantago juncoides, 2–4
Plantago major, 142–43
Pleurotus ostreatus, 78–79
Poison Ivy, xvi–xvii
poisonous snakes, xviii
Polygonum cuspidatum, 126–28
Polygonum persicaria, 47–48

Pontederia cordata, 85–86
Portulaca oleracea, 45–46
Potentilla anserina, 15–16
private land, xix
Prunella vulgaris, 112–13
Pteretis pensylvanica, 22–25
Puffball, 75–77
Purple Trillium, 60–61
Purslane, 45–46

Quickweed, 39–40

Rana catesbeiana, 163–65
Red Spruce, 96–97
Rosa rugosa, 19–20
Rubus spp., 144–45
Rumex crispus (also other *Rumex* species), 29–30

Salicornia spp., 13–14
Salix alba, 98–99
Salix nigra, 98–99
Sarsaparilla, 106–07
Sea Blite, 7–8
Sea-Rocket, 11–12
seasons, xx–xxi
Sedum purpureum, 136–37
Serviceberry, 64–66
Silverweed, 15–16
slow-moving streams, 81
Solidago canadensis, 117–18
spiders, xvii–xix
Spisula solidissima, 175–78
Spotted Joe-Pye Weed, 121
Stinging Nettles, 26–28

Suaeda maritima, 7–8
surf clam, 175–78
swamps, 81
Sweetfern, 150–51

Taraxacum officinale, 152–54
tools, xv
toxic plants, xvi
trees, 91
Trillium undulatum, 60–61
Tsuga canadensis, 94–95
Typha latifolia, 82–84

Urtica dioica, 26–28
Uvularia sessilifolia, 31–32

Vaccinium macrocarpon, 87–89
Valerian, 104–05
Valeriana officinalis, 104–05
Viburnum trilobum, 148–49
Viola papilionacea, 62–63

waste places, 125
weather, xvii
White Pine, 92–93
White Willow, 98–99
Wild Cranberry, 87–89
Wild Oats, 31–32
Wild Raspberries, 144–45
Wild Strawberry, 146–47
Willows, 98–99
Wintergreen, 58–59
Wrinkled Rose, 19–20

Yarrow, 108–09

About the Author

Tom Seymour is a freelance journalist, columnist, book author, musician, Maine guide, water dowser, and naturalist. He writes regular features, including a Maine wildlife column, for *The Maine Sportsman,* Maine's largest outdoor publication. Tom also writes an award-winning outdoor/nature column for *The Republican Journal* and is a regular contributor to *Maine Fish & Wildlife,* the official publication of the Maine Department of Inland Fisheries and Wildlife.

Tom's book credits include *Hiking Maine* and *Fishing Maine,* both by Falcon Press. Tom regularly hosts wild plant walks in and around Waldo County.

Finally, Tom is a professional Highland bagpiper as well as an instructor and composer of pipe music.